COLLINS GEM

ANTIQUE MARKS

Anna Selby
and
The Diagram Group

HarperCollins*Publishers*

HarperCollins Publishers
P.O. Box, Glasgow G4 0NB

A Diagram book first created by Diagram Visual
Information Limited of 195 Kentish Town Road,
London NW5 8SY

First published 1994

Reprint 10 9 8 7 6 5 4 3

ISBN 0 00 470537 8

Printed and bound in Great Britain by
Caledonian International Book Manufacturing Ltd, Glasgow, G64

Introduction

Do you ever attend car boot sales or browse in antique shops in search of bargains? Have you ever wished you knew more about grandma's silver spoon or that old piece of china which has been around your home for so many years? Do you envy the experts' ability to identify and date such fascinating hand-me-downs? If the answer to any of these questions is yes, then *Collins Gem Antique Marks* is for you.

This handy reference work offers a wealth of detailed information which you can refer to at home, yet in a format which is small enough to slip into your bag or pocket. It can always be right at hand, ready to help you seize the chance of 'a good buy', or perhaps to protect you against an unwise purchase.

The book begins with a clear and thorough guide to the hallmarks stamped on British silver and gold ever since the Middle Ages, and those now found on platinum. There follows coverage of the quite different marks to be found on Old Sheffield Plate. A representative selection of Pewter makers' marks is provided next, as an introduction to these once so common household wares. Lastly, the book surveys the vast range of marks to be found on pottery and porcelain, both from Britain and the rest of Europe, and from China and Japan. While the depth of knowledge of the true expert requires years of experience in handling and studying antiques, *Collins Gem Antique Marks* will provide you with the instant means to interpret the marks which are so often crucial in assessing antique objects.

Contents

1. Hallmarks on silver, gold and platinum

Silver and gold have long been prized for their useful and attractive properties. Gold was one of the first metals to be discovered. Being soft and easy to work, colourful, bright and resistant to corrosion, it was ideal for jewellery and other decorative objects. Its scarcity ensured that its value remained high. Silver is harder and less scarce than gold, and thus more widely used in everyday life. Both silver and gold have been mined in Britain since Roman times, in modest quantities. Platinum was unknown in Europe until 1600, only became available commercially in the 19th century, and has only been regulated in Britain since 1975. Used mainly for jewellery, it is more precious than gold. The high value of these three metals makes it essential to have legally enforced standards of purity. The craft of the silversmith has been regulated by Parliamentary Acts and Royal Ordinances since the late 12th century. Since 1 January 1975, a simplified scheme of hallmarks has been in use for British silver, gold and platinum, as directed by the Hallmarking Act of 1973.

PRE-1975 HALLMARKS AND WHAT THEY MEAN

Under the British regulations, any object made of silver or gold is stamped with various 'hallmarks' which enable us to tell when it was made, by whom, where it was manufactured or tested for purity, and, most

important of all, how pure it is. The term 'hallmark' is
derived from Goldsmiths' Hall, the guild hall of the
London Goldsmiths' Company, the body which
oversaw the first assay marks in Britain. In 1300, the
Sterling standard was established at 925 parts of silver
per 1000 in an object, just as in English coinage. No
object was allowed to leave the craftsman's hands until
it had been assayed (tested) and marked with a punch
depicting a leopard's head, a mark which is still used on
London silver. Other assay offices were established in
the English provinces, and in Scotland and Ireland, and
all but the smallest had their own mark of origin.

From 1363, each craftsman was required to add his own
'maker's mark' and to register it.

From 1478, a 'date mark' was required to be struck,
consisting of a letter of the alphabet which signified the
year in which the piece had been assayed. This made it
possible to trace the 'Keeper of the Touch' who had
assayed a particular piece, in case of later disputes as to
purity. It now allows us to determine an accurate date
for any piece of British plate.

A 'duty mark' depicting the head of the current
monarch is found on plate assayed between 1784 and
1890, as proof that a tax on silver goods had been paid
by the maker. The duty mark should not be confused
with later commemorative stamps which mark special
occasions such as Coronations and Jubilees.

Marks of origin on British silver to 1974

The mark of origin, or assay office mark, identifies the
town or city where the item in question was assayed,
and probably manufactured. Since 1300, London has

used the leopard's head (**1**) (sometimes crowned, sometimes not). An exception is the period 1697–1720 when the 'lion's head erased' (**2**) was used, when the Britannia standard replaced the Sterling standard for English silver. At Edinburgh, the earliest Scottish assay office, the mark of origin has always been a three-towered castle (**3**). Dublin has used a harp crowned (**4**) since the mid 17th century. As further examples, Birmingham has long used an anchor (**5**), and Sheffield used a crown (**6**) for many years. More specific information on marks of origin will be found in the introductions to the tables of each city's hallmarks, later in the present chapter.

Sample marks of origin

1   2   3   4   5   6

Makers' marks

Since 1363, silversmiths have been required to stamp their work with a registered mark. Thus one can identify the maker of a particular piece – at least if it was made after about 1666, when the earlier registers at Goldsmiths' Hall were burnt in the Great Fire of London. At first the custom was to use a rebus (for example a picture of a fox for a silversmith whose surname was Fox) and initials combined in one mark. From 1697, makers were required by law to use the first two letters of their surnames (**a, b**), but from 1720 initials again became the norm (**c, d**), sometimes with a symbol added (**e, f**).

In Scotland before about 1700, makers commonly used a monogram (**g**, **h**), but this died out to be replaced by plain initials (**i**). Some used their full surname (**j**). In the case of factories or firms (**k**), the maker's mark is often called the 'sponsor's mark'.

Sample makers' marks

a Thomas Sutton, London 1711
b John Farnell, London 1714
c William Woodward, London 1741
d Mathew Boulton, Birmingham 1790
e John Tuite, London 1739
f Thomas Morse, London 1720
g James Sympsone, Edinburgh 1687
h Robert Brook, Glasgow 1673
i Francis Howden, Edinburgh 1781
j Dougal Ged, Edinburgh 1734
k Lothian and Robertson, Edinburgh 1746

Date letters to 1974

Date letters were introduced in England from 1478, in Scotland (Edinburgh) from 1681, and in Ireland (Dublin) from 1638. The date letter system means that every item of hallmarked silver (and gold) carries a stamp indicating the year when it was assayed. The date stamp takes the form of a letter of the alphabet, changed to the next letter annually in a regular cycle, rather like present-day car registrations. Different assay offices have used different cycles, omitting various letters of the alphabet to form sequences lasting from 19 to 26 years. 'I' was often used for 'J'. Each new cycle was given a new style of lettering and shape of shield, so as to distinguish one cycle from another. The exact day of the year when the letter was changed varied at the different assay offices, and so is given in the introduction to each town later in this chapter.

Sample date letters

1　　　2　　　3　　　4　　　5　　　6

1 London 1561　　**4** Chester 1742
2 London 1936　　**5** Dublin 1662
3 Birmingham 1891　**6** Edinburgh 1968

Standard marks to 1974

In England before 1544, the Sterling silver standard of 92.5% purity (925 parts per 1000) was vouched for by the leopard's head mark of the London Assay Office (**a**). In 1544, Henry VIII debased the coinage to only one third silver, and so a specific 'standard mark' showing a lion passant (**b**) was introduced, to be marked on items which met the Sterling standard. In 1697, the Sterling standard was replaced by the Britannia standard of 95.84% purity (958.4 parts per 1000), to stop the melting down of coins for plate. The Britannia figure (**c**) now replaced the lion passant as the standard mark, and the lion's head erased (**d**) replaced the leopard's head as the mark of origin. From 1720, the Sterling standard and its lion passant mark were reintroduced, but silver of the higher standard (although less common) continued to be marked with Britannia and the lion's head erased right up to 1974. Edinburgh and Glasgow used different standards of fineness (as described on page 38) until 1836, when they adopted the Sterling and Britannia standards.

Sample standard marks

a   **b**   **c**   **d**

Duty marks 1784–1890

Between 1784 and 1890 a duty (tax) was imposed on silver in Britain. To prove that the duty had been paid by the silversmith, an extra mark depicting the head of the current king or queen was struck on most items of silverware produced in England in those years. (In Dublin the duty was imposed only from 1807 and in Glasgow from 1819.) Silversmiths had many tricks to avoid paying duty, so the mark is not always present.

Duty marks

1   **2**   **3**   **4**

1 George III (1760–1820)   **3** William IV (1830–1837)
2 George IV (1820–1830)   **4** Victoria (1837–1901)

Commemorative marks

Special marks have been added in certain calendar years to mark notable occasions. A mark with the heads of both King George V and Queen Mary (**1**) was used to mark their Silver Jubilee in 1935. The Coronation of Elizabeth II in 1953 was commemorated with a mark of the Queen's head (**2**). A similar mark (**3**) was used again to mark her Jubilee in 1977. Special commemorative marks have also been used by the Dublin, Birmingham and Sheffield assay offices to celebrate various anniversaries in the 1970s and 1980s. Because of the exact time of year when the date letter was changed at a particular assay office, such marks may appear not only with the date letter of the year commemorated, but also with that of the year before or the one after.

1 **2** **3**

Marks on foreign silver to 1974

From 1867, a letter F (**a**) was stamped on foreign plate imported into Britain. From 1904, the decimal value of the Sterling (**b**) and Britannia (**c**) standards was marked on imported silver which met those standards, and each assay office had a special mark of origin, as used on imported gold (see page 136), but in an oval shield.

a **b** **c**

THE HALLMARKING ACT OF 1973

In 1973 a new Act of Parliament was passed for regulating and simplifying the law regarding hallmarks on silver, gold and platinum in Britain, and it came into force on 1 January 1975. The Act governs hallmarks at the four remaining assay offices, in London, Edinburgh, Birmingham and Sheffield (but not Dublin, which since 1921 has been the captial of the independent Irish Republic). All items weighing more than 7.8 grams must be hallmarked before they can be described as silver (for gold it is any item above 1 gram, and for platinum above 0.5 gram). There are four hallmarks in total: the registered maker's or sponsor's mark, the standard mark, the mark of origin (assay office mark), and the date letter.

Sample modern silver hallmarks

1 Maker's mark   **2** Standard mark
3 Mark of origin   **4** Date letter

Standard marks from 1975

On Sterling silver, the London, Birmingham and Sheffield Assay Offices still use the traditional lion passant (**a**), while Edinburgh uses the lion rampant (**b**). At all four offices, the Britannia mark (**c**) is used (without the old accompanying lion's head erased) on silver which meets the Britannia standard.

 a   b   c

Marks of Origin from 1975

Only four assay offices remained open in Britain by
1975. London still uses a leopard's head (**1**).
Birmingham still uses its anchor (**2**) and Edinburgh its
three-towered castle (**3**). However, Sheffield has
adopted a York rose (**4**) to replace the crown which it
had used for over 200 years, because the crown risked
being confused with a similar mark on gold. Dublin is
not affected by the Act, and still uses its harp crowned.

1   **2**   **3**   **4**

Date letters from 1975

The date letter now coincides exactly with the calendar
year, it being changed on 1 January every year, and the
same style is used by all four British assay offices.

Imported foreign silver from 1975

The marking of imported foreign silver has been
simplified and standardized under the 1973 Act. The
standard mark consists of the millesimal value in an
oval shield (see below). The marks of origin used by
the four assay offices are similar to those on foreign
gold and platinum, but in an oval shield (see below).

Sterling   Britannia

London   Birmingham Sheffield   Edinburgh

Convention marks

In the past, UK makers had difficulty exporting British silver and gold, because the hallmarks were not legally recognised abroad. Importers faced similar problems. Therefore the European Free Trade Association has produced a convention on the control and marking of precious metals, and the UK has been a signatory since 1976. Under this arrangement, a set of 'convention marks' is commonly recognized. They consist of a common control mark (see below) giving the standard of fineness, the fineness again in numerals, also a mark of origin and a sponsor's (maker's) mark. These marks are struck in place of, or in addition to, the usual British or foreign marks. The system of convention marks means that precious metals assayed in countries which are signatories can be imported and exported between those countries without being re-assayed.

Control marks

750	Gold	18 carat
585	Gold	14 carat
375	Gold	9 carat
925	Silver	Sterling
950	Platinum	

Note that in the UK, any silver below Sterling (925) standard is not approved. Britannia silver and 22 carat gold are not recognized under the convention.

The British Hallmarking Council

A body called the British Hallmarking Council was established under the 1973 Act, and became operative in 1975. The Council coordinates the activities of the four assay offices, without hindering their independence. Its main responsibility is to ensure that adequate assaying facilities are available in the UK, and to see that laws relating to assaying are adhered to.

READING THE HALLMARK CHARTS IN THIS BOOK

Layout of the hallmark charts

The charts on the pages which follow show the hallmarks associated with each of the towns or cities which have had important assay offices, presented in the order in which the assay offices were established. Within each section, all the variations in the design of that city's mark of origin (**b**) and the standard marks (**c** and sometimes **d**) are illustrated, and these are followed by any duty marks or commemorative marks (**e**) and by the date letters (**f**). Unusual marks are fully explained in special feature panels (**a**). Makers' marks are shown separately in lists at the end of each city's section.

For gold, the marks of origin are the same as for silver, except in the cases of Birmingham and Dublin (see pages 134–135). Date letters are the same for gold and platinum as they are for silver.

Note that the hallmark charts apply primarily to silver (as they show the standard marks for silver), but that the same date letters apply equally to British gold.

Here is a sample of a set of marks which you may be looking for (although they may not appear in this order):

In the charts they would be shown as follows:

a Text box for unusual markings
b Mark of origin
c Standard mark
d Possible second standard mark
e Duty or commemorative mark
f Date letter mark
g Text showing year
h Maker's mark (see lists of makers' marks following each city's hallmark charts)

HOW TO READ HALLMARKS

When looking at hallmarks, begin by studying the mark of origin, to find out where the piece was assayed. (If no assay office's mark is present, the piece probably comes from London.) Then turn to the relevant city's section in the tables of hallmarks. Now look at the date letter. This is probably the hardest part of the process. Examine the letter to see whether it is a capital or a small letter, check what kind of script it is in, and note the shape of the shield containing it. Compare these features with the letters in the correct city's tables. Only when you find the example in the table which exactly matches your hallmark can you be confident about its date. Once the place and date of origin are established, it is relatively simple to look up the maker's or sponsor's mark and find out the name of the craftsman or company. Other marks will give extra information, such as whether the piece is Sterling or Britannia silver, whether duty was paid on it, and whether it was made in a Coronation or Jubilee year.

LONDON

The Goldsmiths' Company in London was the first in England authorized to assay and mark gold and silver, after the granting of a Royal Charter in 1327. London has been by far the most important British assay office, both in terms of the high quality of workmanship it maintained, and of the amount and variety of silverware passing through it.

London's mark of origin is a leopard's head, crowned from 1478 to 1821 and thereafter uncrowned. The shape of the head and crown have varied over the years, as has the shield surrounding them. From 1697 until 1720 (while the Britannia standard was in force) the leopard's head was replaced by the lion's head erased and the Britannia mark. From 1784 to 1890, the sovereign's head duty mark was in use.

From 1478 to 1974, London traditionally used a 20-letter sequence (A to U omitting J), with the letter being changed in May each year. Since 1975 all British date letter sequences have been standardized, and are changed on 1 January. In the same year platinum was first assayed and marked here.

The London Assay Office is still in operation.

			0 1551		**b** 1559
G 1544			**O** 1551		**C** 1560
					C 1560
H 1545		**P** 1552		**D** 1561
I 1546		**Q** 1553		
K 1547		**R** 1554		**e** 1562
		S 1555		**f** 1563
L 1548		**T** 1556		**g** 1564
M 1549				**h** 1565
		V 1557		**i** 1566
N 1550				**k** 1567
		a 1558		**k** 1567

1568

 1569

1570

1571

1572

1573

1574

1575

1575

1576

1577

 1578

1579

1580

1581

1582

1583

1584

1585

1586

1587

1588

1589

1590

1591

1592

1593

1594

1595

1596

1597

1598

1599

a 1600	p 1612	f 1623
D 1601	q 1613	g 1624
e 1602	R 1614	h 1625
F 1603	S 1615	i 1626
G 1604	T 1616	k 1627
h 1605	V 1617	l 1628
I 1606	[emblem marks]	m 1629
K 1607	a 1618	n 1630
L 1608	b 1619	o 1631
m 1609	c 1620	p 1632
n 1610	d 1621	q 1633
O 1611	e 1622	r 1634

1635	1646	1657
1636		
1637	1647	1658
1638	1648	1659
1639	1649	1660
1640	1650	1661
1641	1651	1662
1642	1652	1663
1643	1653	1664
1644	1654	1665
1645	1655	1666
	1656	1667

L	1668
M	1669
N	1670
O	1671
P	1672
P	1672
Q	1673
R	1674
S	1675
T	1676
V	1677
a	1678
b	1679
c	1680
d	1681
e	1682
F	1683
g	1684
h	1685
I	1686
k	1687
I	1688
m	1689
n	1690
O	1691
P	1692
Q	1693
r	1694
S	1695
t	1696 1697
A	1697
B	1697

1698	1708	1719
1699	1709	1720
1700	1710	1721
1701	1711	1722
1702	1712	1723
1702	1713	1724
1703	1714	1725
1704	1715	1726
1705	1716	
1706	1717	
1707	1718	

1727

N 1728

From 1716 to 1728, the shield shape for the date letter occasionally varied

O 1729

P 1730

Q 1731

R 1732

S 1733

T 1734

V 1735

 1736

b 1737

c 1738

d 1739

 1739

e 1740

f 1741

g 1742

h 1743

i 1744

k 1745

l 1746

m 1747

n 1748

o 1749

p 1750

 1751

q 1751

r 1752

ſ 1753

t 1754

u 1755

A 1756

B 1757

C 1758

D 1759

E 1760

F 1761

G 1762

H 1763

J 1764

k 1765

L 1766

M 1767

N 1768

O 1769

P 1770

Q 1771

R 1772

S 1773

T 1774

T 1774

U 1775

Two shield shapes for standard mark found, 1776-1795

From 1776 to 1875, a shield without a point was used for some small articles

 a 1776

b 1777

c 1778

d 1779

e 1780	r 1792	H 1803
f 1781	s 1793	I 1804
g 1782	t 1794	K 1805
h 1783	u 1795	L 1806
i 1784		M 1807
k 1785	A 1796	N 1808
l 1786	B 1797	O 1809
m 1787	C 1798	P 1810
n 1788	D 1799	Q 1811
o 1789	E 1800	R 1812
p 1790	F 1801	S 1813
q 1791	G 1802	T 1814

U 1815	k 1825	A 1836
	l 1826	B 1837
a 1816	m 1827	C 1838
b 1817	n 1828	D 1839
c 1818	o 1829	E 1840
d 1819	p 1830	F 1841
e 1820	q 1831	G 1842
f 1821	r 1832	H 1843
	s 1833	I 1844
g 1822	t 1834	K 1845
h 1823	u 1835	L 1846
i 1824		M 1847

1848	1859	1871
1849	1860	1872
1850	1861	1873
1851	1862	1874
1852	1863	1875
1853	1864	
1854	1865	1876
1855	1866	1876
	1867	1877
1856	1868	1878
1857	1869	1879
1858	1870	1880

1881	F
1882	G
1883	H
1884	I
1885	K
1886	L
1887	M
1888	N
1889	O
1890	P

The Queen's head duty mark was not used after 1890

Q	1891
R	1892
S	1893
T	1894
U	1895
a	1896
b	1897
c	1898
d	1899
e	1900
f	1901

g	1902
h	1903
i	1904
k	1905
l	1906
m	1907
n	1908
o	1909
p	1910
q	1911
r	1912
s	1913

t 1914	k 1925	1936 A
u 1915	l 1926	B 1937
a 1916	m 1927	C 1938
b 1917	n 1928	D 1939
c 1918	o 1929	E 1940
d 1919	p 1930	F 1941
e 1920	q 1931	G 1942
f 1921	r 1932	H 1943
g 1922	s 1933	I 1944
h 1923	t 1934	K 1945
i 1924	u 1935	L 1946

M 1947	a 1956	n 1968
N 1948	b 1957	o 1969
O 1949	c 1958	p 1970
P 1950	d 1959	q 1971
Q 1951	e 1960	r 1972
R 1952	f 1961	s 1973
S 1953	g 1962	t 1974
T 1954	h 1963	
U 1955	i 1964	
	k 1965	
	l 1966	
	m 1967	

New letter sequence commenced on 1 January 1975, in accordance with the Hallmarking Act passed in 1973

 1975

B	1976	*M*	1986
		N	1987
C	1977	*O*	1988
		P	1989
D	1978	*Q*	1990
E	1979	*R*	1991
F	1980	*S*	1992
G	1981	*T*	1993
H	1982	*U*	1994
I	1983		
K	1984		
L	1985		

LONDON MAKERS' MARKS

ABS	Adey B Savory	**EC**	Ebenezer Coker
AF **SG**	Andrew Fogelberg & Stephen Gilbert	**EF**	Edward Feline
		ET	Elizabeth Tuite
AS	Thomas Ash	**EW**	Edward Wigan
BC	Benjamin Cooper	**EY**	Edward Yorke
BS	Benjamin Smith	**FC**	Francis Crump
BS **BS**	Benjamin Smith & Son	**FO**	Thomas Folkingham
Bu/BU	Thomas Burridge	**GA**	George Adams
CF	Charles Fox or Crispin Fuller	**GS**	George Smith
		GS **WF**	George Smith & William Fearn
CK	Charles F Kandler (star below)	**GW**	George Wintle
CO	Augustin Courtauld (fleur-de-lys above)	**HA**	Pierre Harache (crown above)
CR	Charles Rawlins	**HB**	Hester Bateman
CR **DR**	Christian & David Reid	**HC**	Henry Chawner
CR **GS**	Charles Reilly & George Storer	**HC** **IE**	Henry Chawner & John Emes
CR **WS**	Charles Rawlins & William Summers	**HN**	Hannah Northcote
		IB	James Bult
DH	David Hennell	**IC**	John Carter
DM	Dorothy Mills	**IG**	John Gould
DPW	Dobson, Prior & Williams	**IH**	John Hyatt
		IL **HL**	John & Henry Lias
DS **BS**	Digby Scott & Benjamin Smith	**IL** **HL** **CL**	John, Henry & Charles Lias
DS **RS**	Daniel Smith & Robert Sharp	**IP**	John Pollock

LONDON MAKERS' MARKS (continued)

Mark	Maker
IS	John Swift or John Scholfield
IW IT	John Walcelon & John Taylor
JA	Joseph Angell
JA JA	J & J Aldous
JC	John Cafe
JE	John Emes
JL	John Lias
LA	Paul de Lamerie (crown and star above)
LO	Nathaniel Lock
LP	Lewis Pantin
MC	Mary Chawner
ME	Louis Mettayer
MP	Mary Pantin
MS	Mary Sumner
MS ES	Mary & Elizabeth Sumner
Ne	Anthony Nelme
NS	Nicholas Sprimont
PB AB	Peter & Anne Bateman
PB AB WB	Peter, Anne & William Bateman
PB IB	Peter & Jonathan Bateman

Mark	Maker
PL	Pierre Platel
PL	Paul de Lamerie (crown and star above, fleur-de-lys below)
PS	Paul Storr
Py	Benjamin Pyne (rose and crown above)
RC	Richard Crossley
RC GS	Richard Crossley & George Smith
R DH H	Robert & David Hennell
RE EB	Rebecca Emes & Edward Barnard
RE WE	Rebecca & William Emes
RG	Robert Garrard
RH	Robert Hennell
RH DH	Robert & David Hennell
RH DH SH	Robert, David & Samuel Hennell
RH SH	Robert & Samuel Hennell
RM RC	Robert Makepeace & Richard Carter

RM **TM**	Robert & Thomas Makepeace
Ro	Philip Rolles
RR	Richard Rugg or Robert Rutland
RS	Robert Swanson
SA	Stephen Adams
Sc	William Scarlett
SC **IC**	S & J Crespell
SG	Samuel Godbehere
SG **EW**	Samuel Godbehere & Edward Wigan
SL	Gabriel Sleath
SM	Samuel Meriton
Sp	Thomas Spackman
S **WI** **A**	Stephen Adams & William Jury
TH	Thomas Heming
TH **IC**	Thomas Hannam & John Crouch
T & W	Turner & Williams
TN	Thomas Northcote
TO	Thomas Oliphant
TP **ER**	Thomas Phipps & Edward Robinson
TP **ER** **JP**	Thomas Phipps, Edward Robinson & James Phipps
TP **IP**	Thomas & James Phipps

TR	Thomas Robins
T **WC** **C**	Thomas & William Chawner
WB	William Burwash
WC	William Cafe
WE	William Eaton or William Eley
WE **CE** **HE**	William, Charles & Henry Eley
WE **GP**	William Eley & George Pierrepont
WE **WF**	William Eley & William Fearn
WF	William Fearn
WF **PS**	William Frisbee & Paul Storr
WG	William Grundy
WI	David Willaume
WP	William Peaston or William Plummer
WRS	W R Smiley
WS	William Sumner or William Smiley
WT	William Tweedie
W **WP** **S**	William Shaw & William Priest

EDINBURGH

Silver was assayed in Edinburgh from the middle of the
15th century, although the first known specimens date
from a century later than that. There was an
Incorporation of Goldsmiths here from at least the
1490s. Over the years Edinburgh has been known
particularly for ecclesiastical and domestic silverware.
The Edinburgh mark of origin is a three-towered castle.
Before 1681 the standard mark took the form of the
Deacon's mark, a monogram of the initials of the
current holder of that office. From 1681 the Deacon's
mark was replaced by the Assay Master's mark, again
consisting of the office-holder's initials. This was
replaced in 1759 by a thistle, which changed in 1975 to
a lion rampant. From 1784 to 1890 the sovereign's head
duty mark was in use.

From 1457 to 1836, Edinburgh used a standard of 916.6
parts of silver per thousand, except in 1489–1555 when
the Standard of Bruges was used (varying from 917 to
946 parts per thousand according to the size of the
object). Only from 1836 was the Sterling standard
adopted at Edinburgh.

Date letters came into use in 1681. Edinburgh generally
used a 25-letter sequence, omitting J (although it was
included in 1789 and 1815). The letter was changed in
October. From 1 January 1975 the standard British date
letter sequence has been used.

The Edinburgh Assay Office is still in operation.
Platinum was first marked here in 1982.

🏯	🇪	1556	🏰	Ⓖ	circa 1617	🏰	1669
🏯	IC	1563	🏰	🐚	1613-1621	🏰	1663-1681
🏯	🐚	1565	🏰	Ⓖ	1616-1635	🏰	1675
🏰	🐚	1575	🏰	🄹	1637	🏰	
🏰	🅰	1576	🏰	🆃	1640	🏰	ⓐ 1681
🏰	🅥	1577	🏰	IF	1642	🏰	
🏰	🅜	1585	🏰	IF	1643		ⓑ 1682
🏰	🅢	1591	🏰	🅰	1644		ⓒ 1683
🏰	🅗	1598	🏰	GC	1649		ⓓ 1684
🏰	🅡	1609	🏰	I•F	1651		ⓔ 1685
🏰	Ⓟ	1611	🏰	ҰB	1660		ⓕ 1686
🏰	IL	1617	🏰	⚭S	1665		ⓖ 1687

h 1688	S 1698	C 1707
i 1689	t 1699	D 1708
k 1690	b 1700	E 1709
l 1691	w 1701	F 1710
m 1692	🏰 P	G 1711
n 1693	t 1702	🏰 EP
o 1694	p 1703	H 1712
p 1695	s 1704	I 1713
q 1696	🏰 P	🏰 EP
🏰 P	A 1705	K 1714
r 1697	B 1706	L 1715
🏰 P	🏰 EP	M 1716

N 1717	V 1725	G 1736
🏰 EP	W 1726	K 1737
O 1718	X 1727	J 1738
P 1719	Y 1728	K 1739
P 1719	Z 1729	🏰 GED
🏰 EP	🏰 AU	L 1740
q 1720	A 1730	M 1741
R 1721	B 1731	🏰 👑 E·L
S 1722	C 1732	N 1742
T 1723	D 1733	O 1743
U 1724	E 1734	🏰 HG
V 1725	F 1735	P 1744

Q 1745	ⓐ 1755	🄺 1764
ⓡ 1746	⒝ 1756	🄻 1765
HG	© 1757	🄼 1766
ⓢ 1747	⒟ 1758	🄽 1767
⒥ 1748	🏰 ⓤ	🄾 1768
ⓤ 1749	© 1759	🄿 1769
ⓥ 1750	⒡ 1760	ⓠ 1770
ⓦ 1751	⒢ 1761	🄡 1771
ⓧ 1752	ⓗ 1762	These alternative town marks are found circa 1771
ⓨ 1753	🏰 ⓤ	
ⓩ 1754	ⓙ 1763	ⓢ 1772
HG	⒥ 1763	🄡 1773

1774		F	1785	P	1795

1774
1775
1776
1777
1778
1779
1780
A 1780
B 1781
C 1782
D 1783
E 1784

F 1785
G 1786-1787
H 1788
I 1789
J 1789
K 1790
L 1791
M 1792
N 1793
N 1793
O 1794
O 1794

P 1795
Q 1796
R 1797
R 1797
S 1798
T 1799
U 1800
V 1801
W 1802

	X	1803					r	1823
	Y	1804		h	1813			
	Z	1805		i	1814		S	1824
				j	1815		t	1825
	a	1806		k	1816			
	b	1807		l	1817		u	1826
	c	1808		m	1818		v	1827
				n	1819		w	1828
	d	1809						
	e	1810		o	1820		x	1829
	f	1811		p	1821		y	1830
	g	1812		q	1822		z	1831

	1832		1844		1856
A	1832	A	1844	Z	1856
B	1833	C	1845		
C	1834	P	1846	A	1857
D	1835	O	1847	B	1858
E	1836	R	1848	C	1859
F	1837	S	1849	D	1860
G	1838	T	1850	E	1861
H	1839	U	1851	F	1862
J	1840	V	1852	G	1863
K	1841	W	1853	H	1864
L	1842	X	1854	I	1865
M	1843	Y	1855	K	1866

🜚 Ⓛ 1867	🜚 Ⓧ 1879
🜚 Ⓜ 1868	🜚 Ⓨ 1880
🜚 Ⓝ 1869	🜚 Ⓩ 1881
🜚 Ⓞ 1870	
🜚 Ⓟ 1871	🜚 ⓐ 1882
🜚 Ⓠ 1872	🜚 ⓑ 1883
🜚 Ⓡ 1873	🜚 ⓒ 1884
🜚 Ⓢ 1874	🜚 ⓓ 1885
🜚 Ⓣ 1875	🜚 ⓔ 1886
🜚 Ⓤ 1876	🜚 ⓕ 1887
🜚 Ⓥ 1877	🜚 ⓖ 1888
🜚 Ⓦ 1878	🜚 ⓗ 1889

🜚 ⓘ 1890
ⓚ 1891
ⓛ 1892
ⓜ 1893
ⓝ 1894
ⓞ 1895
ⓟ 1896
ⓠ 1897
ⓡ 1898
ⓢ 1899
ⓣ 1900
ⓥ 1901

w 1902

r 1903

n 1904

3 1905

A 1906

B 1907

C 1908

D 1909

E 1910

F 1911

G 1912

H 1913

I 1914

K 1915

L 1916

M 1917

N 1918

O 1919

P 1920

Q 1921

R 1922

S 1923

T 1924

U 1925

V 1926

W 1927

X 1928

Y 1929

Z 1930

A 1931

B 1932

C 1933

D 1934

 1935

 1936

1937

1938

1939

1940

1941

1942

1943

1944

 1945

 1946

 1947

 1948

 1949

 1950

 1951

 1952

 1953

 1954

 1955

 1956

 1957

 1958

 1959

 1960

 1961

 1962

 1963

 1964

 1965

1966

 1967

 1968

 1969

 1970

1971

1972

1973-1974

New letter sequence commenced from 1 January 1975, following the Hallmarking Act passed in 1973

 1975

1976

1977

 1978

 1979

 1980

1981

 1982

1983

1984

1985

1986

 1987

1988

 1989

1990

 1991

1992

 1993

 1994

EDINBURGH MAKERS' MARKS

AE	Alexander Edmonstone	**JMc**	John McKay
AG	Alexander Gairdner	**JN**	James Nasmyth
AH	Alexander Henderson	**J&WM**	James & William Marshall
AK	Alexander Kincaid	**LO**	Lawrence Oliphant
AS	Alexander Spencer	**LU**	Leonard Urquhart
AZ	Alexander Zeigler	**MC**	Matthew Craw
CD	Charles Dixon	**M & C**	McKay & Chisholm
E&Co	Elder & Co	**M & F**	McKay & Fenwick
EL	Edward Lothian	**M & S**	Marshall & Sons
EO	Edward Oliphant	**MY**	Mungo Yorstoun
GC	George Christie	**PM**	Peter Mathie
GF	George Fenwick	**PR**	Patrick Robertson
G&K	Gilsland & Ker	**PS**	Peter Sutherland
GMH	George McHattie	**RB**	Robert Bowman
GS	George Scott	**RC**	Robert Clark
HB	Henry Beathume	**RG**	Robert Gordon
HG	Hugh Gordon	**RI**	Robert Inglis
ID	James Dempster	**RK**	Robert Ker
IG	John Gilsland	**WG**	William Ged
IK	James Ker	**W & PC**	William & Peter Cunningham
IR	James Rollo	**WR**	William Robertson
IW	John Walsh	**WS**	Walter Scott
IZ	John Zeigler	**WT IT**	William & Jonathan Taylor
JD	James Douglas		
JM	Jonathan Millidge		

YORK

The assaying of silver in York dates from the mid 16th century. York silver generally followed Scandinavian styles, and is known for pieces of basic design intended for everyday use. From 1717 to 1776 the York Assay Office was closed, and silver made there was assayed at Newcastle.

The York mark of origin was initially a halved leopard's head conjoined with a halved fleur-de-lys in a round shield. In the late 17th century the halved leopard's head was replaced by a halved seeded rose. This mark underwent numerous changes before, in 1701, it was replaced by a new mark depicting five lions passant on a cross, based on the York City coat of arms. From 1700 to 1850 a leopard's head accompanied the lion passant standard mark on York Sterling silver, while the Britannia mark and lion's head erased were used on York Britannia silver. From 1784 to 1856 (when the York Assay Office closed down), the sovereign's head duty mark was in use.

From at least 1607, York generally used a 24-letter date sequence omitting J and U, then from 1787 a 25-letter sequence omitting just J.

	circa 1568
	circa 1577
	circa 1583
	circa 1594

Numerous versions of the town mark (see above) were used at the York Assay Office from c1560 to c1606

F	1564
G	1565
H	1566
K	1568
L	1569

M	1570
O	1572
P	1573
Q	1574
R	1575
S	1576
T	1577
Z	1582
a	1583
b	1584
e	1587
h	1590

k	1592
l	1593
m	1594
n	1595
o	1596
p	1597
q	1598
r	1599
t	1601
x	1604
	circa 1608
	circa 1624

From 1607 to 1630, two versions of the town mark (see previous page) were used at the York Assay Office

[a] 1607

[B] 1608

[C] 1609

[D] 1610

[E] 1611

[F] 1612

[G] 1613

[H] 1614

[J] 1615

[k] 1616

[L] 1617

[M] 1618

[N] 1619

[O] 1620

[P] 1621

[Q] 1622

[R] 1623

[S] 1624

[T] 1625

[U] 1626

[W] 1627

[X] 1628

[Y] 1629

[Z] 1630

From 1631 to 1656, two versions of the town mark (see below) were used at York Assay Office

[a] 1631

[b] 1632

[c] 1633

[d] 1634

[e] 1635

f 1636	w 1653	H 1664
g 1637	x 1654	J 1665
h 1638	y 1655	K 1666
i 1639	z 1656	L 1667
k 1641	🌸	M 1668
l 1642	A 1657	N 1669
m 1643	B 1658	O 1670
o 1645	C 1659	P 1671
s 1649	D 1660	Q 1672
t 1650	E 1661	R 1673
u 1651	F 1662	S 1674
v 1652	G 1663	T 1675

U 1676
V 1677
W 1678
X 1679
Y 1680
Z 1681

From 1682 to 1699, two versions of the town mark (see below) were used at York Assay Office

circa 1680
circa 1696

A 1682
B 1683

C 1684
D 1685
E 1686
F 1687
G 1688
H 1689
J 1690
K 1691
L 1692
M 1693
N 1694
O 1695

P 1696
Q 1697
R 1698
S 1699

A 1700
B 1701
C 1702
D 1703
F 1705
G 1706
A 1708

1711	K 1785	i 1795
1713	L 1786	k 1796
No York plate has been found from the years 1714 to 1777 inclusive		L 1797
	A 1787	M 1798
	B 1788	N 1799
C 1778	C 1789	O 1800
D 1779	c 1789	P 1801
E 1780	d 1790	Q 1802
F 1781	e 1791	R 1803
G 1782	f 1792	In 1803, and again in 1806, the lion passant faced right
H 1783	g 1793	
J 1784	h 1794	S 1804

T 1805	e 1816	r 1828
U 1806	f 1817	s 1829
V 1807	g 1818	t 1830
W 1808	h 1819	u 1831
X 1809	i 1820	v 1832
Y 1810	k 1821	w 1833
Z 1811	l 1822	x 1834
	m 1823	y 1835
a 1812	n 1824	z 1836
b 1813	o 1825	
c 1814	p 1826	A 1837
d 1815	q 1827	B 1838

C 1839
D 1840
E 1841
F 1842
G 1843
H 1844
I 1845
K 1846
L 1847
M 1848
N 1849
O 1850

P 1851
Q 1852
R 1853
S 1854
T 1855
V 1856

York Assay Office
closed in 1856

YORK MAKERS' MARKS

BC **&N**	James Barber, George Cattle, William North	**JB** **GC** **WN**	James Barber, George Cattle, William North
B & N	James Barber, William North	**JB** **WN**	James Barber, William North
Bu	William Busfield	**JB** **WW**	James Barber, William Whitwell
HP **&C**	John Hampston, John Prince, Robert Cattle	**La**	John Langwith
		Ma	Thomas Mangy
IH **IP**	John Hampston & John Prince	**P** **&Co**	John Prince, Robert Cattle
JB **&Co**	James Barber & Co	**RC** **JB**	Robert Cattle, James Barber

NORWICH

The earliest known Norwich silver marks date from the mid 16th century. The city is known principally for ecclesiastical and corporation plate.

The town mark was a lion passant surmounted by a castle. From the early 17th century another town mark was also in use, namely a seeded rose crowned, and variations of both marks appeared until 1701. After 1701, virtually no silver was assayed in Norwich.

Norwich used a 20-letter date sequence (A to V omitting J). The letter was changed each September. There are no recorded makers' marks from Norwich.

A 1565	circa 1600	G 1630
B 1566	circa 1610	H 1631
C 1567	circa 1620	I 1632
D 1568	Several versions of the town marks shown below were used in 1624–1643 (e.g. as above for circa 1620)	K 1633
E 1569		L 1634
F 1570		M 1635
G 1571	A 1624	N 1636
I 1573	B 1625	O 1637
K 1574	C 1626	P 1638
P 1579	D 1627	Q 1639
circa 1590	E 1628	R 1640
circa 1595	F 1629	S 1641

1642

1643

circa
1645

circa
1650

circa
1655

circa
1660

circa
1665

circa
1670

circa
1675

circa
1680

circa
1685

1688

1689

 1691

 1696

 1697

 1701

Little, if any, silver
was assayed at
Norwich after 1701

EXETER

The earliest assay marks date from the mid 16th century. Exeter is known for a good standard of ecclesiastical and domestic silver, but small items were rarely made.

The mark of origin was a round shield containing the letter X surmounted by a crown. After 1701, this was replaced with a three-towered castle. From 1701 to 1720, the Britannia mark and the lion's head erased were in use together as standard marks. After 1721, these were replaced with the leopard's head (omitted from 1777) and the lion passant in square shields. The sovereign's head duty mark was in use from 1784 to 1882.

The date letters began in 1701. Exeter initially used a 24-letter sequence (omitting J and U) then from 1797 a 20-letter sequnce (A to U omitting J). The date letter was changed in August.

Little silver was assayed in Exeter by the end of the 18th century, and the office closed in 1883.

circa 1570	circa 1698	1711
1571		1712
circa 1575	1701	1713
circa 1580	1702	1714
circa 1585	1703	1715
Various town marks were used at Exeter in about 1630	1704	1716
	1705	1717
circa 1635-1675	1706	1718
circa 1635-1675	1707	1719
circa 1680	1708	1720
circa 1690	1709	
circa 1690	1710	1721

🛡X 1722	🛡i 1733	🛡w 1745
🛡Y 1723	🛡k 1734	🛡x 1746
🛡Z 1724	🛡l 1735	🛡y 1747
▪▪▪	🛡m 1736	🛡Z 1748
🛡a 1725	🛡n 1737	▪▪▪
🛡b 1726	🛡o 1738	🛡A 1749
🛡c 1727	🛡p 1739	🛡B 1750
🛡d 1728	🛡q 1740	🛡C 1751
🛡e 1729	🛡r 1741	🛡D 1752
🛡f 1730	🛡s 1742	🛡E 1753
🛡g 1731	🛡t 1743	🛡F 1754
🛡h 1732	🛡u 1744	🛡G 1755

H 1756	U 1768	F 1778
I 1757	W 1769	G 1779
K 1758	X 1770	H 1780
L 1759	Y 1771	I 1781–1782
M 1760	Z 1772	K 1783
N 1761	🛡🛡🦁	L 1784
O 1762	A 1773	M 1785
P 1763	B 1774	N 1786
Q 1764	C 1775	O 1787
R 1765	D 1776	P 1788
S 1766	E 1777	q 1789
T 1767	🛡🦁	r 1790

	p̃ 1791		F 1802		R 1813
	t 1792		G 1803		S 1814
	u 1793		H 1804		T 1815
	W 1794				U 1816
	X 1795		I 1805		
	y 1796		K 1806		a 1817
			L 1807		b 1818
	A 1797		M 1808		c 1819
	B 1798		N 1809		d 1820
	C 1799		O 1810		e 1821
	D 1800		P 1811		f 1822
	E 1801		Q 1812		g 1823

h 1824	S 1834	1843
i 1825	t 1835	1844
k 1826	u 1836	1845
l 1827	1846
m 1828	A 1837	1847
n 1829	B 1838	1848
o 1830	C 1839	1849
	D 1840	1850
p 1831		1851
q 1832	E 1841	1852
	f 1842	R 1853
r 1833		S 1854

1855	1866	1877
1856	1867	1878
	1868	1879
1857	1869	1880
1858	1870	1881
1859	1871	1882
1860	1872	
1861	1873	
1862	1874	
1863	1875	
1864	1876	
1865		

Exeter Assay Office closed in 1883

EXETER MAKERS' MARKS

AR	Peter Arno	**RF**	Richard Ferris
DC	Daniel Coleman	**Ri**	Edward Richards
El	John Elston	**RS**	Richard Sams
FR	Richard Freeman	**SB**	Samuel Blachford
GF	George Ferris	**SL**	Simon Lery
GT	George Turner	**Sy**	Pentycost Symonds
IB	John Buck	**TB**	Thomas Blake
IE	John Elston	**TE**	Thomas Eustace
IP	Isaac Parkin	**TR**	George Trowbridge
IW	John Williams		
JH	Joseph Hicks	**TS**	Thomas Sampson
JO	John Osmont	**Wi**	Richard Wilcocks
JS	John Stone or James Strong	**WP**	William Parry or William Pearse or William Pope
JW	James Williams		
JW & Co	James Whipple & Co	**WRS**	W R Sobey
Mo	John Mortimer	**WW**	William West

DUBLIN

Dublin's Goldsmiths' Company was given its charter in
1638, although silver had been made there long before
and the Sterling standard was adopted as early as 1606.
Dublin silver is known for a high standard of decorative
workmanship.

The mark of origin is a harp crowned. Originally it also
doubled as the standard mark. Up to 1719, two different
versions of the harp crowned may be found, as shown
in the tables. From 1731 the figure of Hibernia was
added to show that duty had been paid. However, from
1807 when the sovereign's head mark was adopted as a
duty mark (up to 1890, as in England), Hibernia was
kept, and in time became regarded as the mark of origin
for Dublin, while the harp crowned came to be regarded
as the Sterling standard mark.

The date letter sequence began in 1638. Dublin used a
20-letter sequence (A to U omitting J) until 1678, when
a 23 or 24-letter sequence was introduced (omitting J, V
and sometimes I). There was an aborted sequence of A
to C in 1717–19. In 1821 a 25-letter sequence was
adopted (omitting J). The date letter was changed in
June until 1932, since when it has changed in January.
As Dublin is in the Irish Republic, it was not affected
by the United Kingdom's Hallmarking Act of 1973.

1638

 1638

A 1638

B 1639

C 1640

D 1641

E 1642

F 1643

G 1644

H 1645

I 1646

K 1647

L 1648

M 1649

N 1650

O 1651

P 1652

Q 1653

R 1654

S 1655

T 1656

U 1657

 1648

@ 1658

b 1659

c 1660

d 1661

e 1662

f 1663

g 1664

h 1665

i 1666

k 1667

l 1668

m 1669

𝖓 1670	𝕿 1680	𝕯 1703
	𝕯 1681	𝕽 1704-1705
𝕺 1671	𝕮𝕰 1682	𝕾 1706-1707
𝕻 1672	𝕱 1683-1684	𝕿 1708-1709
𝖖 1673	𝕲 1685-1687	𝖀 1710-1711
𝖗 1674	𝕳 1688-1693	𝖒 1712-1713
𝕾 1675	𝕶 1694-1695	
𝖙 1676	𝕷 1696-1698	𝖄 1714
𝖚 1677	𝕸 1699	𝖄 1715
	𝕯 1700	𝖅 1716
𝕬 1678	𝕯 1701	
𝕭 1679	𝕻 1702	𝖆 1717

Ⓑ 1718	Ⓚ 1729	Alternative version of the crowned harp used 1739 to 1748
Ⓒ 1719	Ⓛ 1730	
Ⓐ 1720	Ⓛ 1731	Ⓗ 1740
Ⓑ 1721	Ⓜ 1732	Ⓗ 1740
Ⓒ 1722	Ⓝ 1733	
Ⓓ 1723	Ⓞ 1734	Ⓦ 1741–1742
Ⓔ 1724	Ⓟ 1735	Ⓦ 1741–1742
Ⓕ 1725	Ⓜ 1736	Ⓧ 1743–1744
Ⓖ 1726	Ⓡ 1737	Ⓨ 1745
Ⓗ 1727	Ⓢ 1738	Ⓩ 1746
Ⓘ 1728	Ⓣ 1739	
		Ⓐ 1747

B 1748	K 1758	U 1768
C 1749	L 1759	W 1769
D 1750	M 1760	X 1770
E 1751	N 1761	Y 1771
E 1751	O 1762	Z 1772
F 1752	P 1763	A 1773

Alternative version of Hibernia used 1751 to 1752

G 1753	Q 1764	B 1774
H 1754	R 1765	C 1775
I 1757	S 1766	
	T 1767	D 1776
		E 1777

F	1778	R	1789	C	1799
G	1779	S	1790	D	1800
H	1780	T	1791	E	1801
I	1781	U	1792	F	1802
K	1782			G	1803
L	1783	W	1793	H	1804
M	1784	X	1794	I	1805
N	1785	Y	1795	K	1806
O	1786	Z	1796	L	1807
				M	1808
P	1787	A	1797	N	1809
Q	1788	B	1798		

🛡	O	1810	🛡	A	1821	🛡	I	1829
🛡	P	1811	🛡	B	1822	🛡	🛡	
🛡	Q	1812	🛡	C	1823	🛡	K	1830
🛡	R	1813	🛡	D	1824	🛡	🛡	
🛡	S	1814	🛡	E	1825	🛡	L	1831
🛡	T	1815	🛡	e	1825	🛡	M	1832
🛡	U	1816	🛡	F	1826	🛡	🛡	
🛡	W	1817	🛡	🛡		🛡	N	1833
🛡	X	1818	🛡	G	1827	🛡	🛡	
🛡	Y	1819	🛡	🛡		🛡	O	1834
🛡	Z	1820	🛡	H	1828	🛡	P	1835
🛡	🛡		🛡	🛡		🛡	Q	1836

		1837
		1838
		1839
		1840
		1841
		1842
		1843
		1844

		1845
		1846
		1847
		1848
		1849
		1850
		1851
		1851
		1852
		1852

		1853
		1853
		1854
		1855
		1856
		1857
		1858
		1859
		1860
		1861
		1862

S	1863	C	1873	P	1885
		D	1874	Q	1886
t	1864	E	1875	R	1887
U	1865	F	1876	S	1888
V	1866	G	1877	T	1889
W	1867	H	1878	U	1890
X	1868	I	1879	V	1891
Y	1869	K	1880	W	1892
Z	1870	L	1881	X	1893
		M	1882	Y	1894
A	1871	N	1883	Z	1895
B	1872	O	1884		

A	1896	M	1908	D	1919
B	1897	O	1909	e	1920
C	1898	P	1910	F	1921
D	1899	Q	1911	S	1922
E	1900	R	1912	h	1923
F	1901	S	1913	i	1924
G	1902	T	1914	k	1925
H	1903	U	1915	l	1926
H	1904			m	1927
K	1905	A	1916	n	1928
L	1906	b	1917	o	1929
M	1907	C	1918	p	1930-1931

The date letter was changed on 1 June up to 1931. The Q of 1932 and all subsequent letters began on 1 January

 1932

R 1933

S 1934

T 1935

U 1936

V 1937

W 1938

X 1939

Y 1940

Z 1941

A 1942

B 1943

C 1944

D 1945

E 1946

F 1947

G 1948

H 1949

I 1950

J 1951

K 1952

L 1953

M 1954

N 1955

O 1956

P 1957

Q 1958

R 1959

S 1960

T 1961

U 1962

V 1963

W 1964

X 1965

Y 1966

Special 'Sword of Light' mark used to commemorate 50th anniversary of 1916 Rising, in 1966

Z 1967

a 1968

b 1969

c 1970

d 1971

e 1972

F 1973

Special mark used in 1973 showing Gleninsheen Collar, to commemorate Ireland's entry into the EEC

5 1974

h 1975

i 1976

l 1977

m 1978

n 1979

O 1980

P 1981

R 1982

S 1983

T 1984

U 1985

1986

 B 1987

Special shield used in 1987 to commemorate the 350th anniversary of the Goldsmith's Company of Dublin

 C 1988

Special mark used in 1988 to commemorate the Dublin City Milennium Year

 D 1989

 E 1990

F 1991

G 1992

H 1993

I 1994

DUBLIN MAKERS' MARKS

AB	Alexander Brown	**JD**	James Douglas
AL	Antony Lefebure	**JP**	John Power
AR	Alexander Richards	**J.P**	John Pittar
BM	Bartholomew Mosse	**JS**	James Smythe
CM	Charles Marsh	**MH**	Michael Hewitson
CT	Christopher Thompson	**MN**	Michael Nowlan
DE	Daniel Egan	**MW**	Matthew West
DK	David King	**PM**	Patrick Moore
EB	Edward Barrett	**PW**	Peter Walsh
EC	E Crofton	**RC**	Robert Calderwood
EF	Esther Forbes	**RS**	Richard Sawyer
EJ	Edmund Johnson	**RW**	Richard Williams or Robert William
EP	Edward Pome	**SN**	Samuel Neville
GA	George Alcock	**SW**	Samuel Walker
GW	George Wheatley	**TJ**	Thomas Jones
HM	Henry Matthews	**TK**	Thomas Kinslea
IB	John Buckton	**TP**	Thomas Parker
IC	John Cuthbert or John Christie	**TS**	Thomas Slade
IF	John Fry	**TW**	Thomas Walker
IH	John Hamilton	**TWY+**	Edward Twycross
II	Joseph Jackson	**WA**	William Archdall
IL	John Laughlin	**WC**	William Cummins
ILB	John Le Bas	**WL**	William Lawson
IP	John Pittar	**WN**	William Nowlan
IS	James Scott	**WR**	William Rose
		WW	William Williamson

NEWCASTLE

Silver was assayed in Newcastle from the mid 17th century, becoming systematic in 1702. Newcastle is known for domestic silver, tankards and two-handled cups. A curiosity of Newcastle is the presence of three known women silversmiths.

The town mark depicted three separate castles. From 1702 to 1719, the Britannia mark and the lion's head erased were in use. From 1720, these were replaced with the leopard's head and the lion passant. From 1721 to 1727, the lion passant usually faced to the right. The sovereign's head duty mark was used from 1784 to 1883.

The date letter sequence began in 1702. Newcastle used a 19-letter sequence (A to T generally omitting J) until 1759, when a 24-letter sequence was introduced (omitting J and V). The date letter was changed in May. The Newcastle Assay Office was closed in 1884.

circa 1658-1670

circa 1672-1684

circa 1685-1694

circa 1696

circa 1700

 1708

No date marks found for 1709, 1710, 1711, 1713, 1715 or 1716

Various shapes of lions passant and shields were used in 1721–1728. Sometimes the lion faced left

 1712

 1714

 1717

 1718

1719

 1720

 1721

1702

1703

1704

1705

1706

1707

 1722

1723

1724

1725

1726

1727

1728

1729

𝕂	1730	𝐁	1741	𝐎	1753
𝕃	1731	𝐂	1742	𝐏	1754
𝕸	1732	𝐃	1743	𝐐	1755
𝕹	1733	𝐄	1744	𝐑	1756
𝕺	1734	𝐅	1745	𝐒	1757
𝕻	1735	𝐆	1746	𝐒	1758
𝕼	1736	𝐇	1747	🛡️🦁🛡️	
𝕽	1737	𝐈	1748	𝒜	1759
𝕾	1738	𝐊	1749	𝐵	1760–1768
𝐓	1739	𝐋	1750	𝒞	1769
🛡️🦁🛡️	1740	𝐌	1751	𝒟	1770
𝒜	1740	𝐍	1752	�โ	1771

ℱ 1772	ℝ 1783	D 1794
G 1773	S 1784	E 1795
H 1774	T 1785	F 1796
I 1775	U 1786	G 1797
K 1776	W 1787	H 1798
L 1777	X 1788	I 1799
M 1778	Y 1789	1800
N 1779	Z 1790	K 1800
O 1780	A 1791	L 1801
P 1781	B 1792	M 1802
Q 1782	C 1793	N 1803
		O 1804

P 1805	B 1816	O 1828
Q 1806	C 1817	P 1829
R 1807	D 1818	Q 1830
S 1808	E 1819	R 1831
T 1809	F 1820	S 1832
U 1810	G 1821	T 1833
W 1811	H 1822	U 1834
X 1812	I 1823	W 1835
Y 1813	K 1824	X 1836
Z 1814	L 1825	Y 1837
	M 1826	Z 1838
A 1815	N 1827	

A 1839	L 1850	Y 1862
B 1840	M 1851	Z 1863
C 1841	N 1852	(town marks)
D 1842	O 1853	a 1864
E 1843	P 1854	b 1865
F 1844	Q 1855	c 1866
G 1845	R 1856	d 1867
(town marks)	S 1857	e 1868
H 1846	T 1858	f 1869
I 1847	U 1859	g 1870
J 1848	W 1860	h 1871
K 1849	X 1861	i 1872

(k) 1873

Newcastle Assay Office was closed down in 1884

(l) 1874

(m) 1875

(n) 1876

(o) 1877

(p) 1878

(q) 1879

(r) 1880

(s) 1881

(t) 1882

(u) 1883

NEWCASTLE MAKERS' MARKS

AK	Alexander Kelty	**IR**	John Robertson
AR	Anne Robertson	**IS**	John Stoddart
Ba	Francis Batty	**IW**	John Walton
Bi	Eli Bilton	**La**	John Langwith
Bu	John Buckle	**L & S**	Lister & Sons
CJR	Christian Reid Junior	**MA**	Mary Ashworth
		Ra	John Ramsay
CR	Christian & David	**R & D**	Robertson & Darling
DR	Reid		
CR	Christian Reid &	**RM**	Robert Makepeace
IS	John Stoddart	**RP**	Pinkney & Scott
DC	David Crawford	**RS**	
DD	David Darling	**RS**	Robert Scott
DL	Dorothy Langlands	**TP**	Thomas Partis
		TS	Thomas Sewill
DR	David Reid	**TW**	Thomas Watson
FB	Francis Batty	**WL**	William Lister
GB	George Bulman	**WL**	Lister & Sons
IC	Isaac Cookson	**CL**	
IK	James Kirkup	**WL**	
IL	John Langlands	**Yo**	John Younghusband
IR	& John Robertson		
IM	John Mitchison		

CHESTER

From the early 15th century, Chester had a guild of
goldsmiths which supervised the making, assaying and
selling of plate, although marking was not regulated
here until the late 17th century. Chester is known for
small items such as beakers and creamers.

The mark of origin was the city arms, of a sword
between three wheatsheaves (gerbes). From 1701, this
changed to three wheatsheaves halved with three lions
halved. From 1701 to 1718, the figure of Britannia and
the lion's head erased were used as the standard mark.
From 1719, the leopard's head crowned and the lion
passant were used. From 1839, the leopard's head was
omitted. The sovereign's head duty mark was in use
from 1784 to 1890.

The date letter sequence began in 1701, and was of
irregular length, varying from 21 to 25 letters. The
letter was changed each July until 1839, then in August
until 1890, then in July again until the office was closed
down in 1962.

1680	I 1709	U 1720
1690	K 1710	V 1721
STERLING circa 1690-1700	L 1711	W 1722
	M 1712	X 1723
A 1701	N 1713	Y 1724
B 1702	O 1714	Z 1725
C 1703	P 1715	1726
D 1704	Q 1716	A 1726
E 1705	R 1717	B 1727
F 1706	S 1718	C 1728
G 1707	1719	D 1729
H 1708	T 1719	E 1730

F 1731	*S* 1743	C 1753
G 1732	*T* 1744	d 1754
H 1733	*U* 1745	e 1755
J 1734	*V* 1746	f 1756
K 1735	*W* 1747	G 1757
L 1736	*X* 1748	h 1758
M 1737	*Y* 1749	i 1759
N 1738	*Y* 1749	k 1760
O 1739	*Z* 1750	l 1761
P 1740		m 1762
Q 1741	*a* 1751	n 1763
R 1742	*b* 1752	O 1764

P 1765	a 1776	I 1786
Q 1766	b 1777	m 1787
R 1767	c 1778	n 1788
S 1768		o 1789
T 1769	d 1779	p 1790
T 1770	e 1780	q 1791
U 1771	f 1781	r 1792
V 1772	g 1782	s 1793
W 1773	h 1783	t 1794
X 1774		u 1795
Y 1775	i 1784	v 1796
	k 1785	

A 1797	M 1808	B 1819
B 1798	N 1809	C 1820
C 1799	O 1810	D 1821
	P 1811	D 1822
D 1800	Q 1812	
E 1801	R 1813	E 1823
F 1802	S 1814	F 1824
G 1803	T 1815	G 1825
H 1804	U 1816	H 1826
I 1805	V 1817	I 1827
K 1806		K 1828
L 1807	A 1818	L 1829

M	1830	A	1839	
N	1831	B	1840	
O	1832	C	1841	
P	1833	D	1842	
Q	1834	E	1843	
R	1835	F	1844	
S	1836	G	1845	
T	1837	H	1846	
U	1838	J	1847	
		K	1848	
		L	1849	

M	1850
N	1851
O	1852
P	1853
Q	1854
R	1855
S	1856
T	1857
U	1858
V	1859
W	1860
X	1861

Two shield shapes are found for the Sterling mark from 1839 onwards, and also for the date letter from 1900

1862
1863

1864
1865
1866
1867
1868
1869
1870
1871
1872

1873
1874
1875
1876
1877
1878
1879
1880
1881
1882
1883

1884
1885
1886
1887
1888
1889
1890
1891
1892
1893

L	1894	E	1905	R	1917
M	1895	F	1906	S	1918
N	1896	G	1907	T	1919
O	1897	H	1908	U	1920
P	1898	I	1909	V	1921
Q	1899	K	1910	W	1922
R	1900	L	1911	X	1923
[mask] [lion]		M	1912	Y	1924
A	1901	N	1913	Z	1925
B	1902	O	1914	[mask] [lion]	
C	1903	P	1915	a	1926
D	1904	Q	1916	b	1927

1928	
1929	
1930	
1931	
1932	
1933	
1934	
1935	
1936	
1937	

1938	
1939	
1940	
1941	
1942	
1943	
1944	
1945	
1946	
1947	
1948	

Y	1949
Z	1950
A	1951
B	1952
C	1953
D	1954
E	1955
F	1956
G	1957
H	1958

1959

 1961

J	1959
K	1960
L	1961
M	1962

Chester Assay Office closed in August 1962

CHESTER MAKERS' MARKS

B & F	Matthew Boulton & James Fothergill	**JA**	John Adamson
Bi	Charles Bird	**JC**	James Conway or John Coakley
BP	Benjamin Pemberton	**JL**	John Lowe
Bu	Nathaniel Bullen	**JS**	John Sutters
Du	Bartholomew Duke	**NC**	Nicholas Cunliffe
EM	Edward Maddock	**Pe**	Peter Pemberton
FB	Francis Butt	**RG**	Robert Green
GL	George Lowe	**RI**	Robert Jones
GR	George Roberts	**RL**	Robert Lowe
GW	George Walker	**RP**	Richard Pike
IB	James Barton	**RR**	Richard Richardson
IG	John Gilbert	**TM**	Thomas Maddock
IL **TL**	John & Thomas Lowe	**WH**	William Hull
		WP	William Pugh
IR	John Richards	**WR**	William Richardson
IW	Joseph Walley		

GLASGOW

Silver was assayed in Glasgow from the late 17th century, although in the years 1784–1819 Glasgow silverware was mainly assayed in Edinburgh. In the latter year the Glasgow Goldsmiths' Company was formed and several changes were made in the marks. The Glasgow mark of origin was a tree with a bird in the upper branches, a bell hanging from a lower branch and a fish (with a ring in its mouth) laid across the trunk. From 1819, a lion rampant was adopted as the Sterling standard mark, and in 1914 the Scottish thistle was added. Also from 1819, the Britannia standard (and appropriate mark) were in optional use. Up to 1784, the maker's mark was stamped twice, once on each side of the mark of origin. The sovereign's head duty mark was used from 1819 to 1890.

The date letter sequence began in 1681. After about the first 25 years, regular cycles were abandoned and the letters 's' and 'o' were commonly used until 1819, when a full 26-letter sequence was introduced. The date letter was changed annually in July.

The Glasgow Assay Office closed in 1964.

Date letters were used in 1681-1709, but then not again until 1819

The maker's mark was stamped on both sides of the Glasgow town mark up to 1784

  a 1681

 1683

1685

1689

1690

1694

1696

1698

  f 1699

1700

1701

1704

1705

circa 1707

circa 1709

circa 1717

The letter S was used probably as a Sterling mark

 S circa 1728

S circa 1734

 S circa 1743

S circa 1747

S circa 1756

 circa 1757

S circa 1758

E circa 1763

S circa 1773

S circa 1773

O circa 1776

S circa 1780

S circa 1781

S circa 1783

circa 1784

1811

1819 A

1820 B

1821 C

1822 D

1823 E

1824 F

1825 G

1826 H

1827 I

1828 J

1829 K

1830 L

1831 M

1832 N

1833 O

1834 P

1835 Q

1836 R

1837 S

1838 T

1839 U

1840 V

1841 W

1842 X

1843 Y

1844 Z

1845 A

1846 B

1847 C

1848 D

	1849		1860		1871
	1850		1861		1872
	1851		1862		1873
	1852		1863		1874
			1864		1875
	1853		1865		1876
	1854		1866		1877
	1855		1867		1878
	1856		1868		1879
	1857		1869		1880
	1858		1870		1881
	1859				1882

M	1883	Y	1895	1906
N	1884	Z	1896	K 1907
O	1885			L 1908
P	1886	A	1897	M 1909
Q	1887	B	1898	N 1910
R	1888	C	1899	O 1911
S	1889	D	1900	P 1912
T	1890	E	1901	Q 1913
U	1891	F	1902	
V	1892	G	1903	R 1914
W	1893	H	1904	S 1915
X	1894	J	1905	T 1916

U 1917	f 1928	P 1938
V 1918	g 1929	q 1939
W 1919	h 1930	r 1940
X 1920	i 1931	s 1941
Y 1921	j 1932	t 1942
Z 1922	k 1933	u 1943
		V 1944
a 1923	l 1934	W 1945
b 1924	m 1935	X 1946
c 1925		y 1947
d 1926	n 1936	Z 1948
e 1927	o 1937	

𝔄 1949	𝔉 1954
𝔅 1950	ℨ 1955
ℭ 1951	𝔑 1956
	𝔍 1957
𝔇 1952	𝔏 1958
𝔢 1953	𝔐 1959

Ⓝ 1960
Ⓞ 1961
Ⓟ 1962
Ⓡ 1963

The Glasgow Assay Office closed 1964

GLASGOW MAKERS' MARKS

AM	Alexander Mitchell	**JM**	John Mitchell or J Murray
A & T	Aird & Thompson	**LFN**	Luke Newlands
DCR	Duncan Rait	**PA**	Peter Arthur
DMcD	David McDonald	**RG & S**	Robert Gray & Sons
JC	James Crichton	**WP**	William Parkins
JL	John Law		

BIRMINGHAM

The Birmingham Assay Office opened in 1773, after
which the city grew quickly in importance as a centre
for silversmithing.

The mark of origin is an anchor (struck lying on its side
for gold and platinum). It appeared very consistently
with the lion passant standard mark. The sovereign's
head duty mark was in use from 1784 to 1890.

The date letter sequence began in 1773 (in which year
the letter A appeared in three different shapes of
shield). Birmingham used 25 and 26-letter sequences
alternately (omitting J). The date letter was changed in
July until 1975, since when all British date letters have
been standardized and changed on 1 January. In the
same year, platinum was first assayed here.

A special commemorative mark was struck in 1973 to
mark the bicentenary of the Birmingham Assay Office.
The Office is still in operation today.

A 1773
A 1773
A 1773
B 1774
C 1775
D 1776
E 1777
F 1778
G 1779
H 1780
I 1781

K 1782
L 1783
M 1784
N 1785
O 1786
P 1787
Q 1788
R 1789
S 1790
T 1791
U 1792
V 1793

W 1794
X 1795
Y 1796
Z 1797

The duty on silver was doubled in 1797, and so for a short time the King's head was stamped twice

a 1798
b 1799
c 1800
d 1801

e 1802	q 1814	B 1825
f 1803	r 1815	C 1826
g 1804	s 1816	D 1827
h 1805	t 1817	Œ 1828
i 1806	u 1818	F 1829
j 1807	v 1819	G 1830
k 1808	w 1820	H 1831
l 1809	x 1821	J 1832
m 1810	y 1822	K 1833
n 1811	z 1823	L 1834
o 1812		M 1835
p 1813	A 1824	A 1836

⚓ 🦁					
D 1837	A 1849	L 1860
P 1838	B 1850	M 1861
Q 1839	C 1851	N 1862
R 1840	D 1852	O 1863
S 1841	E 1853	P 1864
T 1842	F 1854	Q 1865
U 1843	G 1855	R 1866
V 1844	H 1856	⚓ 🦁
W 1845	I 1857	S 1867
X 1846	J 1858	T 1868
Y 1847	K 1859	U 1869
Z 1848		V 1870

😊 Ⓦ 1871	😊 ⓗ 1882	Ⓡ 1891
😊 Ⓧ 1872		Ⓢ 1892
😊 Ⓨ 1873	😊 ⓘ 1883	Ⓣ 1893
😊 Ⓩ 1874	😊 Ⓚ 1884	Ⓤ 1894
	😊 Ⓛ 1885	Ⓥ 1895
😊 ⓐ 1875	😊 Ⓜ 1886	Ⓜ 1896
😊 ⓑ 1876	😊 Ⓝ 1887	Ⓧ 1897
😊 Ⓒ 1877	😊 Ⓞ 1888	Ⓨ 1898
😊 ⓓ 1878	😊 Ⓟ 1889	Ⓩ 1899
😊 Ⓔ 1879	😊 ⓠ 1890	
😊 Ⓕ 1880	The Queen's head duty mark was not used after 1890	ⓐ 1900
😊 Ⓖ 1881		ⓑ 1901

C 1902	P 1914	⚓ 🦁
d 1903	q 1915	A 1925
e 1904	r 1916	B 1926
f 1905	s 1917	C 1927
g 1906	⚓ 🦁	D 1928
h 1907	t 1918	E 1929
i 1908	u 1919	F 1930
k 1909	v 1920	G 1931
l 1910	w 1921	H 1932
m 1911	x 1922	J 1933
n 1912	y 1923	⚓ 🦁
O 1913	z 1924	👤 K 1934

L 1935	W 1946	F 1955
⚓ 🦁	X 1947	G 1956
M 1936	Y 1948	H 1957
N 1937	Z 1949	J 1958
O 1938	⚓ 🦁	K 1959
P 1939	A 1950	L 1960
Q 1940	B 1951	M 1961
R 1941	⚓ 🦁	N 1962
S 1942	C 1952	O 1963
T 1943	D 1953	P 1964
U 1944	⚓ 🦁	2 1965
V 1945	E 1954	⚓ 🦁

R 1966	(anchor) (lion)	E 1979
S 1967	Z 1974	F 1980
T 1968	New letter sequence commenced from 1 January 1975, in accordance with the Hallmarking Act passed in 1973	G 1981
U 1969		H 1982
V 1970		I 1983
W 1971	(anchor) (lion)	K 1984
X 1972	A 1975	L 1985
In 1973 the bicentenary of the Birmingham Assay Office was commemorated by a special town mark	B 1976	M 1986
	(anchor) (lion)	N 1987
	(head) C 1977	O 1988
	(anchor) (lion)	P 1989
(anchor) (lion)	D 1978	Q 1990
Y 1973		

ℝ 1991	𝕋 1993
𝕊 1992	𝕌 1994

BIRMINGHAM MAKERS' MARKS

C & B	Cocks & Bettridge	**MB**	Matthew Boulton
E & CoLd	Elkington & Co	**MB IF**	Matthew Boulton & John Fothergill
EM & Co	Elkington Mason & Co	**ML**	Matthew Linwood
ES	Edward Smith	**NM**	Nathaniel Mills
ET	Edward Thomasson	**P & T**	William Postan & George Tye
FC	Francis Clark	**REA**	Robinson, Edkins & Aston
GU	George Unite		
GW	Gervase Wheeler	**SP**	Samuel Pemberton
H & T	Hilliard & Thomasson	**T & P**	Joseph Taylor & John Perry
IB	John Bettridge	**TS**	Thomas Shaw
IS	John Shaw	**TW**	Thomas Willmore
IT	Joseph Taylor	**WF**	William Fowke
JW	Joseph Willmore	**Y & W**	Yapp & Woodward
L & Co	John Lawrence & Co		

SHEFFIELD

The Assay Office was opened in 1773. Sheffield is best known for the production of candlesticks.

The mark of origin on Sheffield silver was the crown until 1975, since when it has been a York rose. The standard mark was a lion passant. The sovereign's head duty mark was in use from 1784 to 1890.

From 1780 to 1853, small items were marked with a special stamp on which the crown mark of origin and the date letter were combined.

The application of date letters began in September 1773 with the letter E, changing every July. The choice of letter was quite random until 1824, when Sheffield began to use a regular 25-letter alphabetical sequence (omitting J). In 1975, the standard British date letter sequence was imposed, with the letter being changed on 1 January each year. In the same year, platinum was first assayed at Sheffield.

The Sheffield Assay Office is still in operation.

1773

 1774

 1775

1776

1777

1778

1779

For alternative marks used on small objects from 1780 to 1853, see pages 123-125

 1780

In the period 1780 to 1823, the crown and lion passant varied slightly, eg:

Also varied in years 1824–43, but crown is in a square shield

1781

1782

1783

1784

1785

1786

1787

1788

1789

1790

1791

1792

1793

1794

1795

1796

1797

From 15 July 1797 for nine months, the duty on silver was doubled and so the King's head was stamped twice

V 1798	L 1810	Z 1822
E 1799	C 1811	U 1823
N 1800	D 1812	a 1824
H 1801	R 1813	b 1825
M 1802	W 1814	C 1826
F 1803	O 1815	d 1827
G 1804	T 1816	e 1828
B 1805	X 1817	f 1829
A 1806	I 1818	g 1830
S 1807	V 1819	h 1831
P 1808	Q 1820	k 1832
K 1809	Y 1821	l 1833

m	1834	B	1845	O	1857
P	1835	C	1846	P	1858
q	1836	D	1847	R	1859
r	1837	E	1848	S	1860
S	1838	F	1849	T	1861
t	1839	G	1850	U	1862
u	1840	H	1851	V	1863
V	1841	I	1852	W	1864
X	1842	K	1853	X	1865
Z	1843	L	1854	Y	1866
		M	1855	Z	1867
A	1844	N	1856		

		1868
		1869
		1870
		1871
		1872

From 1780 to 1853, the combined crown and date letters shown below were used on small objects assayed at the Sheffield Office

		1780
		1781
		1782

		1783
		1784
		1785
		1786
		1787
		1788
		1789
		1790
		1791
		1792
		1793
		1794

		1795
		1796
		1797
		1798
		1799
		1800
		1801
		1802
		1803
		1804
		1805
		1806

🙂	S	1807	🙂	v	1819	🙂	h	1831
🙂	P	1808	🙂	Q	1820	🙂	k	1832
🙂	K	1809	🙂	Y	1821	🙂	l	1833
🙂	L	1810	🙂	Z	1822	🙂	E	1834
🙂	C	1811	🙂	u	1823	🙂	P	1835
🙂	D	1812	🙂	a	1824	🙂	q	1836
🙂	R	1813	🙂	b	1825	🙂	r	1837
🙂	W	1814	🙂	c	1826	🙂	S	1838
🙂	O	1815	🙂	d	1827	🙂	t	1839
🙂	T	1816	🙂	e	1828	🙂	u	1840
🙂	X	1817	🙂	f	1829	🙂	V	1841
🙂	I	1818	🙂	g	1830	🙂	X	1842

Z 1843
A 1844
B 1845
C 1846
D 1847
E 1848
F 1849
G 1850
H 1851
I 1852
K 1853

F 1873
G 1874
H 1875
J 1876
K 1877
L 1878
M 1879
N 1880
O 1881
P 1882
Q 1883
R 1884

S 1885
T 1886
U 1887
V 1888
W 1889
X 1890
Y 1891
Z 1892

a 1893
b 1894
c 1895

d 1896	**q** 1908	**b** 1919
e 1897	**r** 1909	**c** 1920
E 1898	**s** 1910	**d** 1921
g 1899	**t** 1911	**e** 1922
h 1900	**u** 1912	**f** 1923
i 1901	**v** 1913	**g** 1924
k 1902	**w** 1914	**h** 1925
l 1903	**x** 1915	**i** 1926
m 1904	**y** 1916	**k** 1927
n 1905	**z** 1917	**l** 1928
o 1906		**m** 1929
p 1907	**a** 1918	**n** 1930

O 1931
P 1932
q 1933
r 1934
s 1935
t 1936
u 1937
V 1938
W 1939
X 1940

y 1941
Z 1942
A 1943
B 1944
C 1945
D 1946
E 1947
F 1948
G 1949
H 1950
I 1951

K 1952
L 1953
M 1954
N 1955
O 1956
P 1957
Q 1958
R 1959
S 1960
T 1961

1962

1963

1964

1965

1966

1967

1968

1969

1970

1971

1972

 1973

The 1773 date letter was used in 1973 to commemorate the Sheffield Assay Office bicentenary

 1974

New letter sequence commenced from 1 January 1975, in accordance with the Hallmarking Act passed in 1973

 1975

1976

 1977

1978

 1979

1980

 1981

1982

 1983

1984

 1985

1986

 1987

O 1988	R 1991	U 1994
P 1989	S 1992	
Q 1990	T 1993	

SHEFFIELD MAKERS' MARKS

AH	Aaron Hadfield	**JC**	J & N Creswick
DH & Co	Daniel Holy & Co	**NC**	
D & S	Dixon & Sons	**JD & S**	James Dixon & Sons
GA & Co	George Ashforth & Co	**JR**	J Round & Son
GE & Co	George Eadon & Co	**MF**	Fenton, Creswick & Co
HA	Henry Archer & Co	**RC**	
H & H	Howard & Hawksworth	**MH & Co**	Martin Hall & Co
HE & Co	Hawksworth, Eyre & Co	**NS & Co**	Nathaniel Smith & Co
HT	Henry Tudor	**RM**	Richard Morton
HW & Co	Henry Wilkinson & Co	**RM & Co**	Richard Morton & Co
IG & Co	John Green & Co	**RM**	Remy Martin &
IH & Co	J Hoyland & Co	**EH**	Edward Hall
IL	John Law	**S & N**	Stafford & Newton
IP & Co	John Parsons & Co	**SR & Co**	Samuel Roberts & Co
IR & Co	John Roberts & Co	**T & IS**	T & I Settle
ITY & Co	John T Younge & Co	**TJ**	TJ & N Creswick
IW & Co	John Winter & Co	**NC**	
JB	James Burbury	**WD**	William Damant
		WF	Fordham &
		AF	Faulkner
		W & H	Walker & Hall

HALLMARKS ON GOLD

Gold marks are much the same as silver marks. A set of gold hallmarks usually consists of four: a mark of origin, a standard mark, a date letter and a maker's mark. Duty marks and commemorative marks are also found at certain periods, just as on silver. Many changes have occurred over the years, most notably with the 1973 Hallmarking Act, which standardized hallmarking at all British assay offices.

Carat numbers

The carat number is the traditional measurement of purity for gold. One carat is equal to one twenty-fourth of the weight of an object. Thus a 22 carat object contains 22 parts gold and two parts alloy. A 9 carat object contains nine parts gold and 15 parts alloy.

Standard marks on British gold

Before 1363, a leopard's head crowned (see **1** on table overleaf) denoted the gold standard of $19^1/_5$ carat, and would be found near the mark of origin on an object. From 1363 onwards, the maker's mark was added to these marks. In 1477, the standard was reduced to 18 carat, but was denoted by the same mark (**1**). In 1478, date letters were first added, as on silver. 1544 saw the first change in the standard mark, to the lion passant (**2**). In 1575 the standard was increased to 22 carat, but using the same mark. In 1798, the 18 carat standard was reintroduced as an alternative, with new marks of a crown and a figure 18 (**3**). The 22 carat standard mark remained the lion passant. From 1844 the lion passant mark was replaced as the standard mark for 22 carat

1		19¹/₅ carat	c1300–1476
		18 carat	1477–1544
2		18 carat	1544–1574
		22 carat	1575–1843
3		18 carat	1798–1974
4		22 carat	1844–1974
5		15 carat	1854–1931
6		12 carat	1854–1931
7		9 carat	1854–1931
8		14 carat	1932-1974
9		9 carat	1932–1974

Scotland

10		18 carat	Edinburgh 1759–1974
11		22 carat	Glasgow 1914–1974

gold by a crown and the figure 22 (**4**). In 1854 three additional lower standards of 15 (**5**), 12 (**6**) and 9 (**7**) carat were introduced, with their standard marks as shown. This was the first time that millesimal numbers (giving the parts of gold per thousand) were used. The

15 and 12 carat standards were dropped in 1932, and replaced by 14 carat (**8**), along with a new mark for 9 carat (**9**). In Scotland up to 31 December 1974, the thistle was used (instead of the crown used in England), with the numbers 18 (**10**) or 22 (**11**) for the 18 or 22 carat gold standards respectively.

Standard marks under the Hallmarking Act 1973
From 1 January 1975, gold standard marks were made the same at all English and Scottish assay offices, becoming a crown mark next to the millesimal value.

 22 carat   14 carat

 18 carat   9 carat

Standard marks on Irish gold
At Dublin from 1637 to 1784, the same marks as used for silver were used for gold, with the standard being set at 22 carat and the mark a harp crowned (**a**). From 1784, there were three standards of 22 (**b**), 20 (**c**) and

a   22 carat   1637–1784

b   22 carat   1784–today

c   20 carat   1784–today

d 18 carat   1784–today

e 14 carat   1935–today

f 9 carat   1854–today

18 (**d**) carat, each using a symbol and number as its mark, as shown. From 1854 three additional lower standards were introduced, of 15 carat (stamped '15' and '.625'), 12 carat (stamped '12' and '.5') and 9 carat (**f**). In 1935, the 15 and 12 carat standards were replaced with 14 carat (**e**), giving the five standards of 22, 20 (rare), 18, 14 and 9 carat found today.

Marks of origin on British and Irish gold

The marks of origin placed on gold by the various assay offices have generally been the same as those placed on silver. However, Birmingham and Dublin have always turned their usual mark on its side in the case of gold. When Sheffield first assayed gold in 1904, it was already using a crown as its town mark for silver. So, to avoid confusion with the crown used as the British standard mark for gold, Sheffield adopted a rose as its town mark on gold. Since 1975 it has used the same York rose on silver and gold alike (see table).

Other marks

Date letters, makers' marks, commemorative marks and duty marks have always been applied to gold just as to silver. Similarly, convention marks for gold follow the same system as on silver (see page 15).

Marks of origin on British and Irish gold

London Birmingham Sheffield Edinburgh Dublin

IMPORTED GOLD
Standard marks on imported gold
From 1904 to 1974, combined carat and millesimal
marks were used. Since 1975, simple millesimal marks
have been used.

Carat	1904–1932	1932–1974	From 1974
22	22 ·916	22 ·916	916
18	18 ·75	18 ·750	750
15	15 ·625	—	—
14	—	14 ·585	585
12	12 ·5	—	—
9	9 ·375	9 ·375	375

Marks of origin on imported gold

From 1876 to 1904, each assay office used its usual mark of origin for gold plus a letter F in an oval or rectangle. From 1904, each office adopted a special mark (as shown below).

	All offices	(1876–1904)
	Birmingham	(1904–today)
	Chester	(1904–1962)
	Dublin	(1904–1906)
	Dublin	(1906–today)
	Edinburgh	(1904–today)
	Glasgow	(1904–1906)
	Glasgow	(1906–1964)
	London	(1904–1906)
	London	(1906–today)
	Sheffield	(1904–1906)
	Sheffield	(1906–today)

PLATINUM

Most platinum comes from Latin America. The metal was unknown in Europe before 1600, and it was not until the 19th century that it was worked into jewellery. In Britain there was no legal requirement to mark platinum until 1975, when the Hallmarking Act of 1973 came into force. There is now a single standard for platinum, set at 950 parts per thousand, and all items weighing more than 0.5 grams must be marked.

As with silver and gold, a set of hallmarks for British platinum consists of four elements: a maker's mark, the standard mark, a mark of origin and a date letter. The platinum standard mark is an orb with a cross on top. Imported platinum also bears four marks, but the standard mark is the figure 950, and the mark of origin used by each assay office has the same symbol as placed on imported silver or gold, but contained in a distinctive roof-shaped shield in the case of platinum.

	British		**Imported**	
	Origin	Standard	Origin	Standard
London				950
Birmingham				950
Sheffield				950
Edinburgh				950

2. Old Sheffield Plate

Old Sheffield Plate was manufactured for about 100 years. It was accidentally discovered in 1742 by Thomas Boulsover, who fused a thin layer of silver onto copper to make an instantly appealing new product that looked like silver but cost a fraction of its price. He used it mainly for small objects such as buttons, snuff boxes and buckles. He tried to keep his process a secret, but it was soon copied and used for everything from candlesticks to teapots.

A problem was soon discovered with Sheffield Plate, in that the silver would wear away and reveal the copper beneath. So from around 1760, a greater proportion of silver to copper was used, although precise standards varied greatly.

The manufacturers of Old Sheffield Plate were often also silversmiths, and all the makers followed popular styles of silverware for their designs. The demise of Old Sheffield Plate was brought about in the 1840s by a new process called British plate, which itself was replaced later in the century by the even cheaper electroplating process.

Marks on Old Sheffield Plate

There are a number of problems with identifying and dating Old Sheffield Plate by its marks. For instance, a precise date cannot be given, as the makers' marks appeared without the date letter that is struck on all solid silver. And, because of the resemblance they bore to silver marks, marks on Sheffield plate were made illegal altogether in 1773. From 1784, marks were again permitted, but had to be easily distinguishable from silver marks. Some manufacturers ignored the new law and used marks looking quite similar to those on silver, some obeyed the letter of the law and others did not bother to use a mark at all.

From 1765 to 1825, the crown was used by some makers as a guarantee of quality. From 1820, some makers stamped an identification such as 'Best Sheffield Heavy Silver Plating' on their products.

Other guidelines

After 1835, electroplating often simulated Sheffield Plate, and later pieces are often passed off as Sheffield Plate even though made by a quite different process. One reliable way of telling Old Sheffield Plate from its imitators is by its colour – it has a soft, slightly bluish glow. The old plating process meant that hollow objects had a seam on them, whereas electro-plating covers a piece seamlessly.

The words 'Sheffield Plated' when marked on an object actually mean it would have been electroplated – the opposite of what one would expect. Something else to watch out for is the foreign competition: cheap French imports of much inferior quality. These are only lightly silvered and have a reddish glow, rather than the bluish one of the genuine article.

MAKERS' MARKS ON OLD SHEFFIELD PLATE

The makers' marks illustrated on pages 140–151 are a selection from the many that are to be found.

Key to abbreviations:

B = Birmingham   L = London
N = Nottingham   S = Sheffield

1   ACLEA
2   A·GOODMAN & CO
3   ALL GOOD
4   ASHFORTH & CO
5   ASH LEY
6   ASKEW MAKER NOTTINGHAM
7   BANI STER
8   BARNET T
9   BEL DON 8
10 BELDON HOYLAND & CO
11 BEST A
12 BEST
13 Bishop Bishop
14 BOULTON
15 BRAD SHAW
16 BRITTAIN WILKIN SON & BROWNILL

MARKS WITH FULL NAMES

1 Lea, Abner Cowel. 1808 B.
2 Goodman, Alexander & Co. 1800 S.
3 Allgood, John. 1812 B.
4 Ashforth, G & Co. 1784 S.
5 Ashley. 1816 B.
6 Askew. 1828 N.
7 Banister, William. 1808 B.
8 Barnet.
9 Beldon, George. 1809 S.
10 Beldon, Hoyland & Co. 1785 S.
11 Best, Henry. 1814 B.
12 Best & Wastidge. 1816 S.
13 Bishop, Thomas. 1830.
14 Boulton. 1784 B.
15 Bradshaw, Joseph. 1822 B.
16 Brittain, Wilkinson & Brownill. 1785 S.
17 Butts, T. 1807 B.
18 Causer, John Fletcher. 1824 B.
19 Cheston, Thomas. 1809 B.
20 Child, Thomas. 1821 B.
21 Needham, C. 1821 S.
22 Cope, Charles Gretter. 1817 B.
23 Corn, James & Sheppard, John. 1819 B.
24 Cracknall, John. 1814 B.
25 Creswick, Thomas & James. 1811 S.
26 Holy, Daniel, Parker & Co. 1804 S.

17 BUTTS

18 CAUSER

19 Cheston

20 CHILD

21 C NEEDHAM
MAKER
SHEFFIELD

22 COPE

23 CORN & Co.

24 CRACKNALL

25 CRESWICKS

26 DAN HOLY PARKER & Cº

1 DAN: HOLY WILKINSON & Cº

2 DAVIS

3 D·HORTON†

4 DEAKIN SMITH & Cº

5 DIXON & Cº

6 DUNN

7 E GOODWIN

8 ELL ER BY

9 F·MOORE

10 FOX·PROCTOR PASMORE·& Cº

11 FREETH

12 FROGGATT COLDWELL & LEAN

13 GAINSFORD

14 GARNETT

15 GIBBS

16 GIL BERT

17 GREEN

18 HALL

MARKS WITH FULL NAMES (continued)

1 Holy, Daniel, Wilkinson & Co. 1784 S.
2 Davis, John. 1816 B.
3 Horton, David. 1808 B.
4 Deakin, Smith & Co. 1785 S.
5 Dixon & Co. 1784 B.
6 Dunn, G B. 1810 B.
7 Goodwin, Edward. 1794 S.
8 Ellerby, W. 1803.
9 Moore, F. 1820 B.
10 Fox, Proctor Pasmore & Co. 1784 S.
11 Freeth, Henry. 1784 S.
12 Froggatt, Coldwell & Lean. 1797 S.
13 Gainsford, Robert. 1808 S.

14 Garnett, William. 1803 S.
15 Gibbs, Joseph. 1808 B.
16 Gilbert, John. 1812 B.
17 Green, Joseph. 1807 B.
18 Hall, William. 1820 B.
19 Hancock, Joseph. 1755 S.
20 Hanson, Matthias. 1810 B.
21 Harrison, Joseph. 1809 B.
22 Harwood, T. 1816.
23 Hatfield, Aaron. 1808 S.
24 Hatfield, Aaron. 1810 S.
25 Hill, Daniel & Co. 1806 B.
26 Hinks, Joseph. 1812 B.
27 Hipkiss, J. 1808 B.
28 Hobday, J. 1829.

19

20

21

22

23

24

25

26

27

28

1 HOLLAND&C°

2 HOR- TON

3 How- ard

4 Hutton

5 H.WILKINSON&C°

6 I.DRABBLE &C°

7 I GREEN&C°

8 I LOVE &C°

9 I &S. ROBERTS.

10 I&IWATERHOUSE&C°

11 J DIXON

12 J. LIN WOOD

13 J.NICHOLDS

14 JONES

15 JOHN PARSONS IC°

16 JOHN SON

17 JOR DAN

18 JOSH.LILLY

19 KIRKBY· FOR·USE

20   LAW

MARKS WITH FULL NAMES (continued)

1 Holland, H & Co. 1784 B.
2 Horton, John. 1809 B.
3 Howard, Stanley & Thomas. 1809 L.
4 Hutton, William. 1807 B.
5 Wilkinson, Henry & Co. 1836 S.
6 Drabble, James & Co. 1805 S.
7 Green, John & Co. 1799 S.
8 Love, John & Co. 1785 S.
9 Roberts, J & S. 1786 S.
10 Waterhouse, J & Co. 1833 S.
11 Dixon, James & Son. 1835 S.
12 Linwood, John. 1807 B.
13 Nicholds, James. 1808 B.
14 Jones. 1824 B.
15 Parsons, John & Co. 1784 S.
16 Johnson, James. 1812 B.
17 Jordan, Thomas. 1814 B.
18 Lilly, Joseph. 1816 B.
19 Kirkby, Samuel. 1812 S.
20 Law, Thomas. 1758 S.
21 Law, John & Son. 1807 S.
22 Lees, George. 1811 B.
23 Lees, George. 1811 B.
24 Lilly, John. 1815 B.
25 Linwood, John. 1807 B.
26 Linwood, Matthew & Son. 1808 B.
27 Love, Silverside, Darby & Co. 1785 S.
28 Mappin Bros. 1850.

21 LAW&SON

22 LEES

23 Lees

24 LILLY&

25 LINWOOD

26 LIN WOOD

27 LOVE SILVERSIDE DARBY & Co.

28 MAP PIN BROT HERS

1 MERE DITH

2 MOORE

3 MORTON & CO

4 N. SMITH & CO

5 PEAKE C

6 PEAR SON

7 PEMBERTON

8 Pim ley

9 F. MADIN & CO

10 Pri me

11 R. LAW.

12 ROBERTS & CADMAN

13 ROD GERS

14 ROGERS

15 RYLAND

16 SAN SOM

17

18 S.C. YOUNGE & CO

19 S C Culmore Patent

20 S. EVANS

MARKS WITH FULL NAMES (continued)

1 Meredith, Henry. 1807 B.
2 Moore, Frederick. 1820 B.
3 Morton, Richard & Co. 1785 S.
4 Smith, N & Co. 1784 S.
5 Peake. 1807 B.
6 Pearson, Richard. 1811 B.
7 Pemberton & Mitchell. 1817 B.
8 Pimley, Samuel. 1810 B.
9 Madin, P & Co. 1788 S.
10 Prime, J. 1839.
11 Law, Richard. 1807 B.
12 Roberts & Cadman. 1785 S.
13 Rodgers, Joseph & Sons. 1822 S.
14 Rogers, John. 1819 B.
15 Ryland, William & Sons. 1807 B.
16 Sansom, Thomas & Sons. 1821 S.
17 Scot, William. 1807 B.
18 Younge, S & C & Co. 1813 S.
19 Colmore, S. 1790 S.
20 Evans, Samuel. 1816 B.
21 Shepard, Joseph. 1817 B.
22 Silk, Robert. 1809 B.
23 Silkirk, William. 1807 B.
24 Small, Thomas. 1812 B.
25 Smith, Isaac. 1821 B.
26 Smith, William. 1812 B.
27 Smith & Co. 1784 S.
28 Staniforth, Parkin & Co. 1784 S.

21 SHEP HARD

22 SILK

23 Sil-kirk.

24 SMALL

25 SMITH

26 SM ITH

27 SMITH&Cº

28 STANIFORTH PARKIN&Cº

1 *Stot*

2 S·TURLEY

3 SYKES & Cº

4 S WORTON

5 THO MAS

6 THOMASON

7 THOˢ LAW & Cº

8 TONKS □

9 TONKS

10 TUDOR ·&·Cº

11 TVR TON

12 TYN DALL

13 WATERHOUSE&Cº

14 WATERHOUSE&Cº

15 WATSON&Cº

16 WATSON PASS&Cº

17 W WATSON
MAKER
SHEFFIELD

18 W BINGLEY

19
W·COLDWELL

20 W GREEN &Cº

MARKS WITH FULL NAMES (continued)

1 Stot, Benjamin. 1811 S.
2 Turley, Samuel. 1816 B.
3 Sykes & Co. 1784 S.
4 Worton, Samuel. 1821 B.
5 Thomas, Stephen. 1813 B.
6 Thomason, Edward & Dowler. 1807 B.
7 Law, Thomas & Co. 1784 S.
8 Tonks, Samuel. 1807 B.
9 Tonks & Co. 1824 B.
10 Tudor & Co. 1784 S.
11 Turton, John. 1820 B.
12 Tyndall, Joseph. 1813 B.
13 Waterhouse & Co. 1807 B.
14 Waterhouse, Hatfield & Co. 1836 S.
15 Watson, Fenton & Bradbury. 1795 S.
16 Watson, Pass & Co. 1811 S.
17 Watson, W. 1833 S.
18 Bingley, William. 1787 B.
19 Coldwell, William. 1806 S.
20 Green, W & Co. 1784 S.
21 Hipwood, William. 1809 B.
22 White, John. 1811 B.
23 Willmore, Joseph. 1807 B.
24 Jervis, William. 1789 S.
25 Linwood, William. 1807 B.
26 Markland, William. 1818 B.
27 Newbould, William & Sons. 1804 S.
28 Woodward, William. 1814 B.
29 Wright & Fairbairn. 1809 S.

21 W·HIP-WOOD

22 WHITE

23 WILLMORE △

24 W JER VIS

25 W·LINWOOD

26 W MARKLAND

27 W·M·NEWBOULD & SONS

28 WOODWARD X

29 WRIGHT & FAIRBAIRN

MARKS WITH INITIALS ONLY

1 Ashforth, Ellis & Co. 1770 S.
2 Hatfield, Aaron. 1808 S.
3 Boulton & Fothergill. 1764 S.
4 Atkin, Henry. 1833.
5 Tudor & Leader. 1760 S.
6 Tudor & Leader. 1760 S.
7 Hancock, Joseph. 1755 S.
8 Littlewood, J. 1772 S.
9 Rowbotham, J & Co. 1768 S.
10 Winter, John & Co. 1765 S.
11 Hoyland, John & Co. 1764 S.
12 Hoyland, John & Co. 1764 S.
13 Smallwood, J. 1823.
14 Roberts, Jacob & Samuel. 1765 S.
15 Morton, Richard. 1765 S.
16 Morton, Richard. 1765 S.
17 Smith, Nathaniel. 1756 S.
18 Roberts & Briggs. 1860.
19 Butts, T. 1807.
20 Briggs, W. 1823.
21 Hutton, W. 1849.

MARKS USING SYMBOLS ONLY

22 Boulton, M & Co. 1784 S.
23 Fenton, Matthew & Co. 1760 S.
24 Watson, J & Son. 1830. Or Padley, Parkin & Co. 1849.
25 Smith, Sissons & Co. 1848.
26 Tudor & Leader. 1760 S.
27 Blagden, Hodgson & Co. 1821.
28 Walker, Knowles & Co. 1840.

22

23

24

25

26

27

28

3. Pewter

Pewter is an alloy of tin with lead, antimony or (notably in the case of fine old pewter) copper. Sometimes bismuth is added to harden the alloy. The proportions of the various metals in the alloy vary greatly, but generally speaking, the more tin, the better the pewter. Britannia metal is a close relative of pewter, and is of high quality, consisting mostly of tin with a small amount of antimony and copper.

Pewter-making began in the Middle Ages, when pewter plates replaced wooden ones, and remained popular into the 19th century, by which time china wares had taken over. A vast amount of domestic pewter ware was produced in Britain, including spoons, flatware, teapots, candlesticks and tankards (for domestic or tavern use), as well as church pewter. Yet, because of its low perceived value and the fact that it was often damaged in daily use, much old pewter has been lost.

As regards design, pewter ware in Britain has generally imitated silverware.

A large quantity of reproduction pewter has been made since the 1920s. Some of this, notably Liberty's Art Nouveau 'Tudric' range, is now quite collectable in its own right. However, most collectors prefer antique pewter, which is characterized by its glowing patina and its higher standards of finish as compared with reproduction pieces. It is the marks to be found on antique pewter which are covered here.

Standards of pewter

The Pewterers' Company regulated the quality of the alloy, in much the same way as the Goldsmiths' Company assayed silver and gold. The three principal types of pewter are, in ascending order of quality:

- Ley pewter: 80% tin, 20% lead
- Trifle pewter: 82% or 83% tin, 17% or 18% antimony
- Plate pewter: 86% tin, 7% antimony, 3.5% copper, 3.5% bismuth

Quality marks

Ley and trifle pewter did not carry any marks of quality. Plate pewter was marked with a letter 'X' (denoting extraordinary ware), sometimes with a crown above it (1), or else it was stamped with the words 'hard metal' or 'superfine hard metal' (2). A rose and crown stamp (3) also indicated fine quality pewter. At first this mark was for export ware only, although by the 18th century it had become more generally used. From the late 17th century, the word 'London' was added to the rose and crown, but it was often used by provincial pewterers also, and so is no guarantee of provenance.

1

3

2

Touch marks

By far the most important marks on pewter are the
'touch marks' or 'touches'. These identify the maker,
and take their name from official 'touch plates' on
which they were stamped when being registered at
Pewterers' Hall. The earliest touch plates dated from
the beginning of the 15th century but were lost in the
Great Fire of London in 1666. The practice of
registering marks on the touch plates began again two
years later and continued until 1824.

The marks do not appear on the touch plates in
chronological order, having been punched in any empty
space in a haphazard fashion. Five copper touch plates
survive at the Pewterers' Company, but the
corresponding register of makers has been lost, making
individual identification impossible in many cases.

A maker's touch mark often consisted simply of his
initials or name, but could also incorporate elaborate
designs, sometimes with a play on words based on the
man's name. Dates also occasionally form part of the
mark, but they indicate the year when the touch was
registered rather than the year the piece was made.

The size of the touch marks varies according to the size
of the item on which they appear, but as a very general
rule, early marks tend to be smaller than later ones.

Other marks

Good early pewter often bears elaborate ownership
marks in a raised form, rather like a wax seal. Triads (a
triangular formation) of letters stamped on the rim of a
pewter plate are generally held to give the initials of the
couple who owned it.

Small marks are also found on pewter in imitation of silver hallmarks, and usually consist of four shields (1). The symbols in the shields generally imitate genuine silver marks quite closely – for instance, the figure of Britannia, the lion passant and the leopard's head – presumably with the purpose of persuading the buyer that the item concerned contained real silver.

After 1826, tankards and measures used in taverns had to carry capacity marks. These were of local design until 1877, after which they were validated by an excise mark consisting of a crown over the monarch's initials and a code number, denoting the area in which inspection of capacity had been carried out (2).

1   **2**

SAMPLE TOUCH MARKS

The touch marks shown on pages 156–159 are a small selection of examples where identification of the maker is possible. They are taken from Touch Plates I and IV at Pewterers' Hall, and serve to illustrate the variety that exists among the hundreds of touch marks registered there. If the touch mark you are seeking is not included, you should consult one of the specialist reference works on pewter marks in your local library. Note that 'master', 'warden', 'steward' and 'yeoman' were ranks and appointments within the guild structure of the Pewterers' Company.

SAMPLE MARKS FROM TOUCH PLATE I

1 'RL' in an oval with a comet between the letters. Robert Lucas, who became a steward of the Pewterers' Company in 1651 and master in 1667.

2 'NK' in a beaded circle with a hand grasping a rose. Thought to be Nicholas Kelk, master in 1665, 1681 and 1686.

3 'SI' in a small beaded circle with a lamb and flag. Probably Samuel Jackson, working in the late 17th C.

4 'WA' in a small circle. Possibly William Austin or William Ayliffe, both working in the late 17th C.

5 'TF' in a beaded oval with a fountain. This is a pun on the maker's name, Thomas Fontaine or Fountain, who took up his livery in 1670.

6 'William Burton' in a beaded circle with a hand holding a sceptre. He was a warden in 1675 and 1680, and master in 1685.

7 'RH' in a beaded circle with a locust, three stars and the date [16]56. Ralph Hulls, warden in 1671 and 1677, master in 1682.

8 'C' in a beaded circle with a crown and cockerel. Another play on a name – Humphrey Cock, who took up his livery in 1679.

9 'John Bull' with a bull's head and two stars in a beaded circle. Late 17th C.

10 'PP' in a circle with a beacon and the date 1668. This could be the mark of Peter Parke or Peter Priest.

11 'SA' in a beaded circle with a lion rampant. Thought to be Sam Atley, who took his livery in 1667.

12 'SQ' in a beaded heart with an arrow and a key with the date [16]73. Thought to be Sam Quissenborough.

1. HENRY MAXTED
2. JOHN KENRICK
3. PHILIP ROBERTS
4. RC
5. I. O. PERRY
6. JOHN HARTWELL
7. JONATHAN LEACH
8. THOMAS GIFFIN
9. A JENNER
10. J. STAPLETON
11. C. SWIFT
12. WOOD HILL

SAMPLE MARKS FROM TOUCH PLATE IV

1 'Henry Maxted' with pillars and the sun shining on a rose. Yeoman 1731.

2 'Iohn Kenrick' with a stork between two pillars. Yeoman 1737, warden 1754.

3 'Philip Roberts' with a lion rampant and a crescent. Yeoman 1738.

4 'RC' in a beaded circle with a lamb holding a crook. Thought to be a play on the name Robert Crooke, yeoman 1738.

5 'I Perry' with a female figure between pillars. Yeoman 1743, warden 1773.

6 'Iohn Hartwell' with a saltire and four castles. Yeoman 1736.

7 'Ionathan Leach' with a quartered shield of arms showing a rose, a sprig of laurel and a lamb and flag. The fourth quarter is illegible. Yeoman 1732.

8 'Thomas Giffin' with a dagger piercing a heart and a ducal coronet, all between pillars. Yeoman 1759.

9 'A Jenner' in a plain rectangle. Thought to be Anthony Jenner, yeoman 1754.

10 'Jno Appleton' with a still and a worm. Yeoman 1768, warden 1799, master 1800.

11 'C Swift' in an indented square with a thistle and a rose (the badge of Queen Anne). Yeoman 1770.

12 'Wood & Hill' with two sheep in a shield. Thought to be Thomas Wood (yeoman 1792) and Roger Hill (yeoman 1791).

Note: 'I' was often used for 'J'. 'Ino' and 'Jno' stand for 'John'.

4. Pottery and porcelain

Unlike the strictly regulated hallmarks which appear on precious metals – and which give today's collector a foolproof means of identification – the marks that appear on pottery and porcelain are a far from reliable guide as to provenance.

Marks may be blurred and impossible to identify. A particular mark – say, an anchor – can indicate a wide variety of periods, factories and countries, and a true attribution can be given only by looking at the weight, colour, shape and pattern of the piece itself. The size and colour of the mark, as well as the way it was made, also have a bearing on its identification. Often marks have been used which imitated those of famous factories – for example there were endless copies of the Meissen crossed swords. Marks have also been added fraudulently at later dates.

If a piece of pottery bears no mark at all, it does not mean the piece is necessarily of an early date, because much pottery from every period bears no mark at all. Confusion may also result from the fact that a mark may refer to a factory, to a potter or painter who worked there, or to a past owner of the piece. Dates, too, are not to be taken at face value, because they rarely give the date of actual manufacture. When incorporated into a mark, a date commonly indicates the year when the factory was established, or when a particular design was introduced. However, the design registration marks which were applied from 1842 do give reliable dates for British wares thereafter. There were also a few factories which employed their own reliable dating systems, notably Sèvres, Derby, Minton and Wedgwood.

Pottery and porcelain are best understood by looking and touching, and the more you see and handle the various wares, the more of a feel you will get for them. Once you are more confident in your knowledge of the wares themselves, marks can be used as a very useful back-up. Nevertheless, approaching marks with a good deal of healthy suspicion is always to be recommended!

Pottery types

Pottery is made simply of clay, but many additions have been made to the clay mix to give added strength, and decorative glazes have been applied to enhance appearance. The following types are among the most common and important:

- *Creamware*: earthenware with a cream-coloured glaze, giving something of the impression of porcelain.
- *Delft*: Earthenware with a tin glaze, made in the 17th and 18th centuries.
- *Faïence*: Tin-glazed earthenware.
- *Majolica*: Decorative tin-glazed earthenware first made in 15th century Italy and copied in the 19th century.
- *Stoneware:* A strong non-porous ware made from adding sand or flint to the clay.
- *Ironstone*: Patented by Charles James Mason in 1813, using slag from iron furnaces to strengthen the wares.

Porcelain types

Porcelain was first made in China from the vital
ingredients of kaolin (China clay) mixed with petuntse
(China rock). It is recognized by its strength, its
musical note when struck, and its translucent delicacy.
From the moment porcelain was first imported in the
15th century, it was a huge success in Europe and there
were many attempts made to reproduce it in the West.
The ingredients for the hard paste porcelain of the
Chinese original were eventually found at Meissen in
what is now Germany, and porcelain production began
there in the early 18th century. The process was then
imitated throughout Europe.

Other experiments to imitate porcelain produced soft-
paste porcelain, which has a less hard, glittery glaze
than hard-paste porcelain, as well as less strength.

METHODS OF APPLYING MARKS

The way in which a mark is made can help in
attributing it to a particular factory (as can its colour).
Where relevant, this has been noted in the pages which
follow. There are four main methods:

● *Incising*: This is one of the earliest and simplest
methods, whereby a mark is scratched into the clay
before it is fired.

● *Impressing:* A stamp is used to press a mark into the
unfired clay.

● *Underglaze painting or transfer-printing*: Until 1850,
this appeared only in blue, after which other colours
were used. As the name suggests, the mark was made
before the final glaze was applied over it.

● *Overglaze marks*: These may be painted, transfer-printed or stencilled onto finished wares. This method is a particularly easy one for forgers to imitate.

A thumbnail guide to establishing dates

- A printed mark signifies post-1800 manufacture
- Marks which include the royal arms appeared only after 1810
- Marks including the name of a pattern are also post-1810, and often much later
- The diamond registration mark indicates the period 1842–83 (see page 164)
- 'Limited' or 'Ltd' denotes 1860 onwards
- 'Trade mark' signifes 1862 onwards
- The practice of using 'Royal' followed by the manufacturer's name began in the mid 19th century
- 'Rd No' (Registered Number) was introduced in 1884
- The word 'England' was used from 1891 and 'Made in England' from early in the 20th century

REGISTERED DESIGN MARKS

The system of Registered Designs was devised in 1839 to protect the design of industrial products in much the same way that the patent laws protect inventions. There were two early layouts of Registration Marks, one in use from 1842 to 1867, the other from 1868 to 1883.

Mark layout 1842–67

Class (for pots)
Year
Month
Day
Bundle

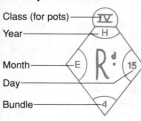

Year codes 1842-67	
A 1845	N 1864
B 1858	O 1862
C 1844	P 1851
D 1852	Q 1866
E 1855	R 1861
F 1847	S 1849
G 1863	T 1867
H 1843	U 1848
I 1846	V 1850
J 1854	W 1865
K 1857	X 1842
L 1856	Y 1853
M 1859	Z 1860

Mark layout 1868–83

Class (for pots)
Day
Bundle
Year
Month

Year codes 1868-83	
A 1871	K 1883
C 1870	L 1882
D 1878	P 1877
E 1881	S 1875
F 1873	U 1874
H 1869	V 1876
I 1872	X 1868
J 1880	Y 1879

Month codes 1842–83

The same system of code letters was used to indicate the month of registration on both types of design mark layout shown opposite.

A	December	E	May	K	November
B	October	G	February	M	June
C/O	January	H	April	R	August
D	September	I	July	W	March

REGISTRATION NUMBERS

From 1884, the complex diamond-shaped registration mark was replaced by a simple registration numbering system. The abbreviation 'Rd No' (for Registered Number) often appeared before the number. The system remains in use today. The dates of numbers used in the early years are given in the table below.

Rd No	Year	Rd No	Year
1	1884	291241	1897
19754	1885	311658	1898
40480	1886	331707	1899
64520	1887	351202	1900
90483	1888	368154	1901
116648	1889	385088	1902
141273	1890	402913	1903
163767	1891	425017	1904
185713	1892	447548	1905
205240	1893	471486	1906
224720	1894	493487	1907
246975	1895	518415	1908
268392	1896	534963	1909

1

2

3

4

5

6

7

8

9

10

11 Aaron Wood.

12 ADAMS

13 AMERICAN POTTERY C° o o o JERSEY CITY N J

14 Ariello

15 AVALON

A

1 Paris, France. Painted red/gold. c1795.

2 Bow, London, England. Red. c1765.

3 Sèvres, France. Mark and date letter for 1753. Date letters ran alphabetically until 1793 (AA from 1778) appearing inside or alongside the 'crossed Ls' in blue (or later red) enamel.

4 Sèvres, France, 1778.

5 Nymphenberg, Germany. Impressed or incised. c1745.

6 Arras, France. Soft-paste porcelain. 1770–90.

7 'De Ster' (The Star), artist A Kiell. Delft, Holland. c1763.

8 Helene Wolfsohn, decorator. Meissen, Germany. c1860.

9 Meissen, Germany. Painted underglaze blue. c1725.

10 Thomas Allen (painter). Wedgwood. 1875–1905.

11 Burslem, Staffordshire, England. Impressed. c1750.

12 Adams & Co, Tunstall, England. From c1790.

13 New Jersey, USA. Printed. Mid 19th C.

14 Capo-di-Monte, Italy. Incised. c1760.

15 Cartwright Bros, East Liverpool, Ohio, USA. 1880–1900.

1 *B*

2

BARR FLIGHT & BARR.
Royal Porcelain Works.
WORCESTER.

London-House.
N°1 Coventry Street.

3

4 *+B*

5

6

7 B & G

8 · B · H ·

9 *BL*

10 *M*

11 B.S. & T.

12 BELPER POTTERY
DENBY

14 *Booth*

13 *6 Compot*

15 *Bristoll*

B

1 Flight & Barr, Worcester, England. Scratched in clay. 1793–1800. The most common Worcester marks are crescents, the letter W and copies of Chinese and Meissen marks.

2 Worcester. Printed. 1807–13. Later Worcester wares carry the full name.

3 Lille, France. Faïence. 1720–88.

4 Bristol, England. Painted. c1773.

5 Sèvres, France. 1754.

6 Bristol, England. 1773.

7 Bing & Grondahl, Copenhagen, Denmark. 1853.

8 Knoller, Bayreuth, Germany. Faïence. c1730.

9 Limbach, Germany. Porcelain. Late 18th C.

10 Niderviller, France. 1744–80.

11 Barker, Sutton & Till, Burslem, Staffordshire, England. 1830-50.

12 Belper Pottery, Derbyshire, England. Stoneware. 1812.

13 'De Vergulde Bloompot' (The Golden Flowerpot), Delft, Holland. c1693.

14 Enoch Booth, Tunstall, Staffordshire, England. Impressed. c1750.

15 Bristol, England. Porcelain. c1750.

1. C
2. C
3. C
4. C
5. C
6. C
7. CB
8. CB
9. ✳ CB
10. OB
11. CD
12. S
13. C G W
14. C M +
15. ▷ Chelsea 1745
16. Chamberlain's

C

1 Nantes, France. c1780.

2-6 Caughley, England. Variations of the Caughley mark, printed or painted in underglaze blue between 1772–95.

7 Bayreuth, Germany. Painted. 1744.

8 Castel-Durante, Italy. c1570.

9 'De Ster' (The Star), C D Berg, Delft, Holland. c1720.

10 Coalport, Coalbrookdale, England. Hard-paste porcelain. Painted blue. c1825–50.

11 Limoges, France. Hard-paste porcelain. c1783.

12 Coalport, Coalbrookdale, England. Hard paste porcelain. Painted blue. Early 19th C.

13 Leeds, England. c1760.

14 St Cloud, France. Faïence/porcelain. c1711.

15 Chelsea, London, England. Soft-paste porcelain c1745.

16 Worcester, England. Red. 1788–1808.

D

1 Davenport, England. Impressed. 1793–1882.
2 Derby, England. 1770–84.
3 Caughley, England. Hard-paste porcelain. Painted blue. c1750.
4 Derby, England. Soft-paste porcelain. Red. c1756.
5 John Donaldson (painter), Worcester, England. Porcelain. c1770.
6 Derby (Chelsea), England. c1782.
7 Coalport, Coalbrookdale, England. Painted blue. c1825–50.
8 William Littler, potter, Longton Hall, Staffordshire, England. 1750–60.
9 Louis Dorez, Nord, France. c1735.
10 Proskau, Silesia, Germany. Faïence. 1770–83.
11 'De Paauw' (The Peacock), Delft, Holland. Faïence. c1700.
12 Derby, England. Incised. c1750.
13 Limoges, France. c1875.
14 Castleford, England. Pottery. Impressed. c1790.
15 J van Duyn, 'De Porceleyne Schootel' (The Porcelain Dish), Delft, Holland. Faïence. Painted blue. c1764.

1 *E*

2 *E*

3 *E*
1779

4 **EB**

5 *Ef*

6 E. I. B.

7 E. L
1754

8 E
M+B
J760

9 E. Borne
1689

10 ENGLAND

11 ENOCH BOOTH
1757

12 Enoch Wood

13 E. NORTON
BENNINGTON
VT.

14

15

E

1 Elton Pottery, Somerset, England. 1880–90.

2 St Petersburg, Russia. 1762–96.

3 Derby, England. 1779.

4 Paris, France. c1800.

5 Moustiers, France. Faïence. 18th C.

6 Hanley, England. Impressed. 18th C.

7 Bow, London, England. c1754.

8 Michael Edkins and his wife, Bristol, England. Blue. c1760.

9 Henri Borne, Nevers, France. c1689.

10 From 1891, the word 'England' appeared on English wares.

11 Tunstall, Staffordshire, England. c1757.

12 Burslem, England. Impressed, moulded or incised. 1784–90.

13 Bennington, Vermont, USA. Impressed. c1882.

14 Ernst Teichert, Meissen, Germany. Late 19th C.

15 E Jacquemin, Fontainebleu, France. 1862–66.

1 *f*

2 *f*

3 *F*

4 *F*

5 *F*

6 *F.*

7 F B

8 FBB

9 *ff*

10 F Z

11 Fatto en Torino

12 Flight & Barr
Worcester
Manufacturers to their
Majesties

F

1 Rouen, France. Faïence. c1644.
2–3 Variations of mark of Furstenberg, Germany. 1760–70.
4 Jacob Fortling, Copenhagen, Denmark. Faïence. 1755–62.
5–6 Variations of mark of Bow, London. 1750–59.
7 Francois Boussemart, Lille, France. c1750.
8 Flight, Barr & Barr, Worcester. 1813–40.
9 Rouen, France. 1673–96.
10 Buen Retiro, Madrid, Spain. Soft-paste porcelain. c1759.
11 Turin, Italy. Faïence. 16th C.
12 Flight & Barr, Worcester, England. 1792–1807.
13–14 Variations of Worcester Flight marks. 1782–91.
15 Bordeaux, France. 1781–87.
16 Fulper Bros, Flemington, New Jersey, USA. Impressed. 19th C.

1 G

2 g

3 G

4 $\#G$

5 G^x

6 a

7 G

8 a

9 arrow with G

10 Sardin

11 G D M

12 G.H. & co.

13

G

1 Bow, London, England. Porcelain. 1744–60.
2 Bow, London, England. Porcelain. 1750–70.
3–4 Tavernes, France. Faïence. 1760–80.
5 Faenza, Italy. 15th C. The town of Faenza gave its name to faïence.
6 Buen Retiro, Madrid, Spain. Soft-paste porcelain. 1759–1808.
7 Gotha, Germany. Hard-paste porcelain. Painted blue. 1775–1800.
8 Gotha, Germany. Painted blue. 1805–30.
9 Unger, Schneider, Thuringia, Germany. 1861–87.
10 Nicolas Gardin, Rouen, France. c1760.
11 Limoges, France. 1842–98.
12 Swansea, Wales. 1765–1870.
13 Emile Galle, Nancy, France. Early 20th C.
14 Guy Green, printer, Liverpool, England. 1756–99.
15 Limoges, France. c1773.
16 Alcora, Spain. Faïence/ porcelain. c1750.

14 GREEN

15 GR et Cie

16 GROS

1 h

2 h

3 H

4 $\mathcal{H}.$

5 H

6 HB

7

8 HDC

9 $H.L.$

10 $h z z$

11 HK

12 $H.P.$

13 HP 1636

14 HARTLEY, GREEN & CO.

H

1–2 Hannong, Faubourg St Lazare, Paris, France. c1773.

3 Strasburg, Germany. Faïence/porcelain. c1750.

4 Nevers, France. Faïence. 17th C.

5 D Hofdick, 'De Ster' (The Star), Delft, Holland. Faïence. c1705.

6 Antoine de la Hubaudiere, Quimper, France. c1782.

7 Faincerie de la Grande Maison, Quimper, France. c1898–1902.

8 Delft, Holland. Faïence. 17th C.

9–10 Hannon & Laborde, Vincennes, France. c1765.

11 Prague, Germany. Porcelain. 1810–35.

12 Humphrey Palmer (potter), Hanley, England. c1760.

13 Winterthur, Switzerland. Faïence. 17th C.

14 Leeds, England. Pottery. c1750.

15 Hugo Booth, Stoke-on-Trent, England. c1785.

16 Henry Roudeburth, Montgomery, Pennsylvania, USA. Early 19th C.

15

H. BOOTH

16

Henry Roudeburth

April ‖ 28ᵗ̇ʰ 1811

1 I

2 ✛I✛
   ✛

3 I·B

4 iB *

5 I.C.

6 I.E.1697

7 I.W

8 IE:W:1699:
WROT:HAM

9 I.Smith

10 IRESON

11 I. & G.
RIDGWAY

12 IRONSTONE
B & M

13 I.SEYMOUR
TROY

14 I.B.FARRAR & SONS

I

1 Bow, London, England. Painted red or blue. 1744–59.

2 St Cloud, France. Faïence/porcelain. 1678–1766.

3 Bristol, England. Painted blue or gold. 1770–81.

4 'De Ster' (The Star), Delft, Holland. Faïence. Painted blue. c1764.

5 John Crolius, New York, USA. Impressed. c1790.

6–8 Variations on mark from Wrotham, England. Slipware. 17th or 18th C.

9 Joseph Smith, Wrightstown, Pennsylvania, USA. c1775.

10 Nathaniel Ireson (potter), Wincanton, England. Tin-glazed earthenware. 1740–50.

11 Job Ridgway, Hanley, Staffordshire, England. Earthenware. 1802–8.

12 Bagshaw & Meir, Burslem, Staffordshire, England. Earthenware. Printed or impressed. 1802–8.

13 Israel Seymour, Troy, New York, USA. Impressed. c1825.

14 Isaac Farrar, Fairfax, Vermont, USA. c1800.

15 J Dale(potter), Burslem, Staffordshire, England. Late 18th C–early 19th C.

16 Lisbon, Portugal. c1773.

15 I.DALE BURSLEM   **16** IAG 9

1 J

2 J

3

4 " F "

5 JA

6 Φ C'

7 JE

8 &HS

9 J. & W R.

10 J M F

11 J P.

12 J. P.
    L

13 J. R.

14 R

15 Jw D

J

1 Longton Hall, Newcastle, England.
Porcelain/stoneware. 1750–60.

2 Ilmenau, Thuringia, Germany. Faïence/porcelain.
c1777.

3 Ilmenau, Thuringia, Germany. 1900–40.

4 Copenhagen, Denmark. 1750–60.

5 Aprey, France. Faïence. c1750.

6 J Dimmock & Co, Hanley, Staffordshire, England.
Late 19th C.

7 G Jones & Sons, Stoke-on-Trent, England. Late
19th C–early 20th C.

8 James Hadley & Sons, Worcester, England.
1896–1903.

9 Bell Works, Shelton, England. Pottery. Printed.
1770–1854.

10 St Cloud, France. Soft-paste porcelain. 1678–1766.

11 Jacob Petit (potter), Fontainebleu, France. Hard-
paste porcelain. Painted blue. c1800.

12 Jean Pouyat (potter), Limoges, France. Painted red.
1842.

13 John Remney, New York, USA. Stoneware. c1775.

14 Joseph Robert (potter), Marseilles, France.
Porcelain. 1754–93.

15 Ashby Potters Guild, Burton-on-Trent, England.
Pottery. Early 20th C.

1 K

2 K

3 K

4 K

5 K.H.
P.A

6 K.H.C.W

7 K.P.M

8 K.P.M.

9 Keeling Toft & Co.

10 K & G
LUNEVILLE

11 KIEBZ
13
II

12 Kishere

13 KLUM

K

1 Klosterle, Bohemia, Germany. Porcelain, lead-glazed earthenware. 1794–1803.

2 Jan Kuylich, Delft, Holland. Faïence. Painted blue. 17th C.

3 Jan Kuylich the younger, Delft, Holland. Faïence. Painted blue. Registered 1680.

4 Kiel, Germany. Faïence. c1770.

5 Meissen, Germany. Hard-paste porcelain 1720–60.

6 Königliche Hof Conditorei, Meissen, Germany. Hard-paste porcelain. Painted blue. 1720–60.

7 Königliche Porzellan Manufaktr, Meissen, Germany. Hard-paste porcelain. Underglaze blue. c1723.

8 Krister, Germany. 19th C.

9 Keeling (potter), Hanley, Staffordshire, England. Impressed. 1806–24.

10 Keller & Guerin (owners), Luneville, France. Faïence. 1778.

11 Kiev, Russia. Porcelain. 1798–1850. Stoneware. 1800–11.

12 Joseph Kishere (potter), Mortlake, England.

13 Klum, Germany. Porcelain. 1800–50.

14 Smith-Phillips China Co, East Liverpool, Ohio, USA. Late 19th C.

15 Knowles, Taylor & Knowles, East Liverpool, Ohio, USA. Established 1854.

14

KOSMO

15 K.T. & K.
CHINA

1   2   3   4

L   *L*   *L*   ⚡

5   6   7

L   *L*   *L*

8   9   10

L   *L*   Lo✠

11   LEEDS POTTERY

12   LEEDS · POTTERY
     LEEDS · POTTERY

L

1–3 Jean-Joseph Lassia (proprietor), Paris, France. Porcelain. 1774–84.
4 Lille, France. Hard-paste porcelain. Late 18th C.
5 Tours, France. Faïence. c1756.
6 Valenciennes, Nord, France. Faïence. 1735–80.
7 Limbach, Thuringia, Germany. Hard-paste porcelain. Painted red. c1772.
8 Buen Retiro, Spain. Soft-paste porcelain. 1759–66.
9 Valenciennes, Nord, France. Faïence, hard-paste porcelain. c1785.
10 St Cloud, France. Faïence, porcelain. 1678–1766.
11–13 Leeds, England. Creamware. Late 18th C.
14–16 Limbach, Thuringia, Germany. Late 18th C.

13

LEEDS ✿ POTTERY

14   **15**

16

13

MASON'S PATENT
IRONSTONE CHINA

M

1–2 Rouen, France. 1720–30.
3–4 Minton, Stoke-on-Trent, England. Underglaze blue. 1800–30.
5 Longton Hall, Newcastle, Staffordshire, England. 1750–60.
6–7 Pierre Roussencq (founder), Marans, France. Faïence. Late 18th C.
8 Moreau Aîné, Limoges, France. Late 19th C.
9 Arnoldi, Germany. Early 19th C.
10 Mennecy, France. Porcelain. 1734–73.
11 Herculaneum, Liverpool, England. 1833–41.
12 Schmidt Brothers, Germany. Late 18th C.
13 Mason, Fenton, England. Faïence. Printed. 1813.
14 Meissner Porzellan Manufaktur, Dresden, Germany. Hard-paste porcelain. c1723.
15 Minton & Boyle, Stoke-on-Trent, England. Impressed. 1836–41.
16 Mayer & Newbold (potters), Hanley, England. Early 19th C.

15 M&B

FELSPAR PORCELAIN

16 M. & N.

1 N **2** N **3** N

4 N **5** N **6** U
+

8 X
5 **9**

7 N

N.H.

10
NⱱR **11** Nantgarw

12 NEWCASTLE

13 New Hall **14** NOTTN.
1703

N

1 Niderviller, France. Faïence. Mid to late 18th C.
2 Derby, England. Incised blue or red. c1770.
3 New Hall, Shelton, England. Painted red. 1782–1810.
4 New Hall, Shelton, England. Painted black. 1782–1810.
5 Nove, Venice, Italy. 1800–25.
6 Limbach, Germany. Porcelain. Late 18th C.
7 Wrotham, England. 17th C.
8 Bristol, England. Pottery, porcelain. Overglaze blue or gold. 18th C.
9 Urbino, Italy. Pottery. 16th C.
10 Christian Nonne & Roesch (owners), Ilmenau, Thuringia, Germany. Porcelain. c1786.
11 Nantgarw, Wales. Hard-paste porcelain. Painted red. c1811.
12 Newcastle-upon-Tyne, England. Pottery. Impressed. c1800.
13 New Hall, Shelton, England. Painted red. Late 18th C.
14 Nottingham, England. Pottery. c1705.
15 Niderviller, France. Faïence. Mid to late 18th C.
16 Bassano, Italy. Soft-paste porcelain. c1760.

1 O

2 O G

3 O B

4 O P.

5 O S

6 [mark]

7 O. V.

8 O Y.

10 OLDFIELD & CO.

9 O. & B.

11 OLIVER
A PARIS

12 Opaque China

13 Opaque China
B. B. & I.

14 ORIENTAL
STONE
J. & G. ALCOCK

15 Orleans

16 OWENS
UTOPIAN

○

1 Bow, London, England. Porcelain. c1750.

2 St Petersburg, Russia. Porcelain. c1760.

3 Mennecy-Villeroy, France. Porcelain, faïence. Mid 18th C.

4 Mennecy-Villeroy, France. Porcelain, faïence. Painted blue. c1773.

5 George Oswald (painter and potter), Ansbach, Bavaria, Germany. 1692–1733.

6 Oscar Schlegelmilch, Thuringia, Germany. Late 19th C.

7 Ohio Valley China Co, Wheeling, West Virginia, USA. c1890.

8 Olerys & Laugier (managers), Moustiers, France. Hard- and soft-paste porcelain. c1739.

9 Ott & Brewer, Trenton, New Jersey, USA. c1880.

10 Brampton, England. Brownware. c1825.

11 Olivier (potter), Paris, France. Faïence. Late 18th C.

12 Cambrian, Wales. Earthenware. c1807.

13 Baker, Bevans & Irwin, Swansea, Wales. c1830.

14 J & G Alcock, Cobridge, England. Mid to late 19th C.

15 Duke of Orleans (patron), Loiret, France. Mid 18th C.

16 J B Owens Pottery Co, Zanesville, Ohio, USA c1890.

1 P

2 P

3 P

4 P

5 P

6 P

7 P.

8 P

9 P

10 P

11 PA

12 AI

13 BI

14 II

15 P. P. Coy. L.
Stone China

16 poupre
d japonng

P

1–2 Seth Pennington (potter), Liverpool, England.
Painted gold or colour. Late 18th C.

3–4 James & John Pennington (potters & painters),
Liverpool, England. Painted gold or colour. Mid
18th C.

5–6 Pinxton, Derbyshire, England. Soft-paste
porcelain. 1796–1813.

7 St Cloud, France. Faïence, porcelain. Mid 18th C.

8 Nymphenberg, Germany. Porcelain. Impressed or
incised. Mid 18th C.

9 Philippe-Auguste Petit (potter), Lille, France. Painted
colour. c1778.

10 Pigory (owner), Chantilly, France. Soft-paste
porcelain. Early 19th C.

11 Rouen, France. Faïence. Painted colour. 16th or
17th C.

12 Moustiers, France. Faïence. Mid 18th C.

13 Paul Hannong (proprietor), Strasburg, France.
Underglaze blue. 1740–60.

14 Paris, France. 1786–1793.

15 Plymouth, Pottery Co, Plymouth, England. c1850.

16 Moulins, France. Faïence. c1730.

1 R

2 R

3 R

4 R

5 R

6 R

7 R

8 R

9 R B

10 R

11 R

12 RAINFORTH & CO.

13 Rockingham

14 R Hancock fecit

R

1 Louis-François Roubiliac (sculptor), Chelsea, London. Impressed. c1738.

2 Bristol, England. Porcelain. c1750.

3 Marseilles, France. Porcelain. 1773–93.

4 Bow, London, England. Porcelain. 1750–60.

5 Joseph Gaspard Robert (potter), Marseilles, France. Faïence. 1754–93.

6–7 Rauenstein, Thuringia, Germany. Porcelain. 1783.

8 Rouen, France. 16th–17th C.

9 Bow, London, England. Porcelain. 1750–60.

10 Sèvres, France. Hard- and soft-paste porcelain. Painted blue, gold. 1793–1804.

11 Meissen, Germany. Hard-paste porcelain. Underglaze blue c1730.

12 Rainforth (potter), Leeds, England. Late 18th or early 19th C.

13 Rockingham, Swinton, Yorkshire, England. Late 18th or early 19th C.

14 Worcester, England. Hard-paste porcelain. 1756–1774. 'Made by R Hancock'.

15 William Reid (potter), Liverpool, England. Porcelain. Impressed. 1755–59.

16 Ralph Toft (potter), Wrotham, England. Slipware. c1677.

15

Reid & Co.

16 RALPH TOFT

S

1 St Petersburg, Russia. Hard-paste porcelain. Painted blue. c1744.

2–3 Caughley, England. Hard-paste porcelain Painted blue. 1755–99.

4 Rouen, France. Faïence. c1760.

5 St Cloud, France. Faïence, porcelain. 1678–1766.

6 Eisenach, Germany. Mid to late 19th C.

7 Schlaggenwald, Bohemia, Germany. Porcelain. 1793–1866.

8 Joseph Flower (painter), Bristol, England. Delft. 1739–51.

9–10 Jacques Chapelle (potter), Penthieve factory, Sceaux, Seine, France. Soft-paste porcelain. 1749–63. Later 'Sceaux' painted in blue.

11 Caughley, England. Porcelain. 1750–1814.

12 Smith, Ambrose & Co, Burslem, Staffordshire, England. c1800.

13 John Sadler (engraver), Liverpool, England. Pottery and hard- paste porcelain. Printed. 1756–70.

14 Caughley, England. Porcelain. Impressed. 1750–1814. Caughley factory taken over in 1799 by Coalport.

15 Spode. Stoke-on-Trent, England. Porcelain. Impressed. Painted red, blue, black or gold. c1770.

16 Spode & Copeland, Stoke-on-Trent, England. 1770–97.

1 2 3 4

5 6 7

8 9

Tannova

10

T. FELL & CO.

11

T. FLETCHER & CO.

ThoMAS

12

TOFT

13

Théodore Haviland

Limoges

FRANCE

T

1–3 Thomas Frye (manager), Bow, London. Porcelain.
1744–59.

4 Tebo (modeller), Bristol, England. Porcelain.
1770–75.

5 Tite Ristori, Nevers, France. Pottery. c1850.

6 Torquay, Devon, England. Terracotta. 1875–1909.

7 Nevers, France. Faïence. 18th C.

8 T Vickers, Lionville, Pennsylvania, USA. c1805.

9 Tannowa, Bohemia, Germany. Faïence, porcelain.
1813–80.

10 Thomas Fell (potter), Newcastle, England. c1817.

11 T Fletcher (owner), Shelton, England. 18th C.

12 Thomas Toft (potter), Burslem, England. Slipware.
c1670.

13 Theodore Haviland, Limoges, France. c1920.

14 Theodore Haviland, New York, USA. Printed green
or black. c1936.

15 Warne & Letts, South Amboy, New Jersey, USA.
c1806.

16 Theodore Deck, Paris, France. Faïence. c1859.

14

THEODORE HAVILAND
NEW YORK

15 T.W.J.L.

16 HD

1. U. & C.

2. U k C

3. V

4. V & B M

5. V

6. V

7. ★ V

CHELSEA

8. V R

9. V R

10. V^e M & C

11. Ven^d

12. VILLEROY & BOCH

13. Velazg^z

14. V C ▫

U/V

1 J Uffrecht, Haldensleben, Germany. Late 19th C.
2 Sarreguemines, France. Faïence, porcelain, c1770.
3 Nathaniel Hewelcke (potter), Venice, Italy. Porcelain.
Incised. 1757–63.
4 Villeroy & Boch, Mettlach, Saar, Germany.
1890–1910.
5 Charles Vyse, Chelsea, London. Early 20th C.
6–7 Veuve Perrin (potter), Marseilles, France. Faïence.
Painted black. c1790.
8 Jan van der Kloot, Delft, Holland. Faïence. Painted
blue. c1765.
9 Baron Jean-Louis Beyerle, Niderviller, France.
Faïence. 1754–70.
10 Rue Thiroux factory, Paris, France. Hard-paste
porcelain. c1775.
11 Venice, Italy. Hard-paste porcelain. c1700.
12 Villeroy & Bosch (potters), Mettlach, Germany.
Faïence. c1842.
13 Buen Retiro, Spain. Hard-paste porcelain.
1759–1808.
14 Alcora, Spain. Porcelain, faïence. Mid 18th C.
15 Varages, France. Faïence. 18th C.
16 Vinovo, Italy. Porcelain. Underglaze blue or incised.
c1775.

15   **16**

W

1 Plymouth, England. Hard-paste porcelain painted blue. c1768.

2 Plymouth, England. Painted red, blue, gold. c1768.

3 Thomas Wolfe (potter), Stoke-on-Trent, England. Impressed. 18th–19th C.

4–8 Variations of the Worcester mark. Hard-paste porcelain, 1775–83.

9 Rouen, France. Faïence. c1720.

10–11 Wegeley (founder), Berlin, Germany. Porcelain. 1751–60.

12 Bristol, England. c1853.

13 Chelsea, London, England. Porcelain. 1745–84.

14–15 Variations of the Worcester mark. Late 18th C.

16 Absolon (enameller), Yarmouth, England. c1800.

14

15

16

1 *Walton*

2 W. & B.

3 Wedgwood

4 WEDGWOOD

5 WEDGWOOD & CO

6 Wedgwood & Co.

Ferry bridge

7 WEDGWOOD
ENGLAND

8 WEDGWOOD Z W

9 WINCANTON

10 XX

11 XX

12 X E

13 Z

14 Z

W, X, Y, Z

1 John Walton (potter), Burslem, England. Earthenware. 18th–19th C.

2 Wedgwood & Bentley, Staffordshire, England. Earthenware. 1769–80.

3 Wedgwood, Etruria, England. Pottery. Impressed. c1771.

4 Wedgwood, Etruria, England. Impressed on pottery, 1771. Printed red, blue, gold on porcelain, 1812–6.

5–6 Ralph Wedgwood, Ferrybridge, England. Stoneware. Impressed. 1796–1800.

7 Wedgwood. Pottery. After 1891.

8 Wedgwood. Pottery. Impressed. After 1780.

9 Wincanton, Bristol, England. Earthenware. 17th C.

10–11 Vaux (or Bordeaux), France. Hard-paste porcelain. Late 18th C.

12 'De Griekse A' (The Greek A), Delft, Holland. c1674.

13–15 Zurich, Switzerland. Pottery, Hard-paste porcelain. Painted blue. Late 18th C.

16 Worcester. 1775–85.

15

16

ANCHORS

1–4 Chelsea, London, England. Porcelain. Underglaze blue, gold. 1750–69.

5 Chelsea, London, England. Soft-paste porcelain Painted gold or red. c1745.

6 Chelsea, London, England. Soft-paste porcelain. Underglaze blue or red, blue, purple. 1749–56.

7 Derby-Chelsea, England. Porcelain. Painted blue, lilac or gold. c1770.

8 Derby, England. Porcelain. c1745.

9 Bow, London, England. Hard-paste porcelain. Painted red or blue. c1744.

10 Bow, London, England. Soft-paste porcelain. Painted red or brown. c1760–80.

11–12 Bow, London, England. Soft-paste porcelain. Painted red, brown or blue. c1760–80.

13 Bow, London, England. Porcelain. 1745–70.

14 Liverpool, England. Cream earthenware. 1793–1841.

15 Sceaux factory, Seine, France. Porcelain, faïence. c1775.

16 Thomas Fell (potter), Newcastle, England. Impressed. 18th–19th C.

14   **15**   **16**

1

2

3

4

5

6

GRIFFIN

7

8

9

Baguley
Rockingham Works.

10

BELLEEK

11

TRADE MARK

WEDGWOOD & Co.

12

ANIMALS, FISHES AND INSECTS

1 Furstenberg, Germany. Porcelain. 18th C.
2 Hesse Cassel, Germany. Hard-paste porcelain.
Painted blue. c1763.
3 Oiron, France. 16th C.
4 'De Klauw" (The Claw), Delft, Holland. Mid 18th C.
5 Edgem Malkin, Burslem, England. Late 19th C.
6 Williamson, Longton, England. Early 20th C.
7 Frankenthal, Bavaria, Germany. Hard-paste
porcelain. Painted blue. c1754.
8 Amsterdam, Holland. Hard-paste porcelain. Painted
blue. c1772.
9 Rockingham, Swinton, England. Hard-paste
porcelain. Painted red. c1824.
10 Belleek, Ireland. c1860.
11 Ralph Wedgwood, Burslem, England. 1796–1800.
12 Lille, France. Hard-paste porcelain. Stencilled and
painted red. c1784.
13–14 Nyon, Switzerland. Hard-paste porcelain.
Underglaze blue. c1780.
15 Seville, Spain. Glazed pottery. 19th C.

ARROWS

1–5 Bow, London, England. Porcelain. c1750.
6 Plymouth, England. Hard-paste porcelain. Painted blue. 1768–70.
7–8 Leeds, England. Pottery. Impressed. c1774.
9–11 Caughley, England. Hard-paste porcelain. Painted blue. Mid–late 18th C.
12 Derby, England. Porcelain. c1830.
13 Derby, England. Porcelain. 1745–1848.
14 Robert Allen (painter), Lowestoft, England. Porcelain. 1757–80.
15 W Absolon (enameller), Yarmouth, England. Porcelain, earthenware. Impressed. Early 19th C.
16 Rue de la Roquette factory, Paris, France. Hard-paste porcelain. Painted blue. c1774.
17 La Courtille factory, Paris, France. Hard-paste factory. Underglaze blue, incised. c1771.

BIRDS

1–2 Ansbach, Bavaria, Germany. Hard-paste porcelain. Painted blue. c1765.

3 J V Kerckof (artist), Amsterdam, Holland. 1755–70.

4–5 Herculaneum factory, Liverpool, England. c1833.

6 Charles Ford, Burslem, England. 19th C.

7 Boulton, Machin & Tennant, Tunstall, England. Late 19th C.

8 T Rathbone, Tunstall, England. Early 20th C.

9 Limoges, France. 1842–98.

10 Sèvres, France. Hard-paste porcelain. Painted red. c1810.

11 Sèvres, France. Hard-paste porcelain. c1852.

12 Homer Laughlin China Co, East Liverpool, Ohio USA. Late 18th C.

13 W H Goss, Stoke-on-Trent, England. Late 19th C.

14 T Mayer, Stoke-on-Trent, England. c1829.

15 Florence, Italy. Faïence. Late 19th C.

16 Hanks & Fish, Swan Hill Pottery, South Amboy, New Jersey, USA. c1849.

15

16

1

2

3

4

5

6

7

8

9

10

11

E.WOOD & SON BURSLEM.
SEMI CHINA
WARRANTED

12

F N
J

13

ORLEA
C·M·B·N
·V·S

CIRCLES

1–2 Faenza, Italy. Faïence. 16th–17th C.

3 Spode, Stoke-on-Trent, England. Impressed. Late 18th C.

4 Hochst, Germany. Hard-paste porcelain. Painted blue, red, gold. 1750–65.

5–6 Worcester, England. Hard-paste porcelain. Underglaze blue. Late 18th C.

7 Bow, London, England. Soft-paste porcelain. Late 18th C.

8 Ken & Binns, Worcester, England. Porcelain. 1852–62.

9 Wedgwood & Bentley, Etruria, England. 1769–80.

10 Charles Field Haviland Co, Limoges, France. c1882.

11 Enoch Wood & Sons, Burslem, England. c1790.

12 Ilmenau, Germany. Porcelain. 19th C.

13 Orleans, France. Hard-paste porcelain. c1800.

14 Urbino, Italy. Pottery. 16th C.

15 Cologne, Germany. Pottery. 17th C.

16 Minton, Stoke-on-Trent, England. Hard-paste porcelain. Printed. 1800.

14

15

16

SALOPIAN

CRESCENTS

1–2 Bow, London, England. Porcelain. c1750–75.
3–7 Caughley, England. Painted blue. c1775–99.
8–11 Worcester, England. Hard-paste porcelain.
c1751–1800.
12 Nymphenburg, Germany. Porcelain. Impressed or
incised. Mid to late 18th C.
13 Pinxton, England. Soft-paste porcelain. 1796–1801.
14 Turkey. Porcelain. c1850.
15 Munden, Germany. Faïence. 18th C.
16 Faenza, Italy. Faïence. 16th C.

13

14

15

16

LINES AND CROSSES

1 St Petersburg, Russia. Hard-paste porcelain. Painted blue. Late 18th C.

2 Royal Copenhagen Factory, Copenhagen, Denmark. 1830–45.

3 Royal Copenhagen Factory, Copenhagen, Denmark. c1775.

4 Varages, France. Faïence. c1770.

5–6 Bristol, England. Porcelain. Painted colour. c1770.

7 Leeds, England. Painted colour. c1770.

8 Chelsea, London, England. Porcelain. 1745–84.

9 Nymphenburg, Germany. Porcelain. Impressed or incised. Late 18th C.

10 Bow, London, England. Mid 18th C.

11 Copenhagen, Denmark. c1770.

12–14 Bow, London, England. Mid 18th C.

15 Meissen, Germany. 19th C.

16 Longton Hall, Staffordshire, England. 1749–60.

17 Caughley, England. 1775–99.

15   **16**   **17**

CROSSED SWORDS

1–8 Marks from the Meissen factory in Germany, all painted blue.
1 Early 18th C.
2–3 c1730.
4–6 Mid 18th C.
7–8 c1723.
9 Worcester, England. Mid 18th C.
10 Bristol, England. Porcelain. Painted blue, gold. Mid 18th C.
11 Derby, England. Mid 18th C.
12 Coalport, Coalbrookdale, England. Early 19th C.
13 Samson, Edme, Paris, France. Late 19th C.
14 Caughley, England. Painted blue. 1775–99.
15 Jacob Petit, Fontainebleu, France. 1830–40.
16–17 Bristol, England. Porcelain. Painted blue or gold. 1773–81.

CROWNS

1 Derby, England. 1775–70.
2 Bloor, Derby, England. 1811–48.
3 Vincennes, France. Hard-paste porcelain. c1765.
4 Derby, England. Painted red or violet. c1780–4.
5 Belleek, Ireland. Late 19th C.
6 Worcester, England. c1813–40.
7 Derby, England. c1784–1815.
8 Royal Crown Derby, Derby, England. 1877–9.
9 Sèvres, France. 1773.
10 Sèvres, France. 1824–30.
11 Meissen, Germany. 1720–50.
12 Leeds, England. Earthenware. Mid 18th C.
13–14 St Petersburg, Russia. Porcelain. Painted colour.
Late 18th C.
15 Herculaneum, Liverpool, England. Impressed or
printed. 1800–41.
16 James Clews (potter), Cobridge, England.
Earthenware. Blue printed. c1819–29.

14   15   16

CURVES

1–5 Sèvres, France. Soft-paste porcelain. 1745–53.
6–8 Sèvres, France. Soft- and hard-paste porcelain. 1764–71.
9 Worcester, England. Mid 18th C.
10 Minton, Stoke-on-Trent, England. 18th C to 1831.
11 Coalport, Coalbrookdale. Porcelain. Early 19th C.
12–13 Buen Retiro, Madrid, Spain. 1759–1808.
14 Niderviller, France. Late 18th C.
15 Nuremburg, Germany. Early 18th C.
16 Nymphenburg, Germany. c1747.

FLEURS-DE-LYS

1 St Cloud, France. Soft-paste porcelain. Impressed. c1680–1766.

2 Rouen, France. Faïence. Painted colour. 16th C.

3 Bow, London, England. Soft-paste porcelain. Painted blue. c1730.

4–5 Marseilles, France. Faïence. Late 18th C.

6–8 Buen Retiro, Madrid, Spain. Soft-paste porcelain. 1759–1808.

9–10 Ginori, Italy. Painted blue. 1820–50.

11 Minton, Stoke-on-Trent, England. Painted green. After 1850.

12 Capo di Monte, Naples, Italy. 1730–40.

13 Orleans, France. 1753–1812.

14–15 Lowesby, England. Mid 19th C.

FLOWERS AND TREES

1–4 'De Roos' (The Rose), Delft, Holland. Late 17th C.
5 Longport, Staffordshire, England. c1825.
6 Rose & Co, Caughley, England. Hard-paste porcelain.
Painted colour. 1799.
7 Coalport, Coalbrookdale, England. Early 19th C.
8 Volkstedt factory, Thuringia, Germany. Porcelain.
Late 18th C.
9 Greuby Faïence Co, Boston, Mass., USA, c1900.
10 Imenau, Germany. Faïence, porcelain. Late 18th C.
11 Limbach, Thuringia, Germany. Porcelain. Late
18th C.
12–13 Grosbreitenbach, Germany. Hard-paste
porcelain. Painted colour. Late 18th C.
14 Berlin, Germany. Hard-paste porcelain. Painted
blue, green or gold. c1800. Often on damaged pieces.
15 Delft, Holland. Faïence. 18th C.
16 'De Ster' (The Star), Delft, Holland. Faïence.
c1720.

14

15

16

1

2

3

4

5

6

7

8

9

10 W. & B. Lt.

11 PORCELAINE OPAQUE TRADE MARK

12 ENOCH WOOD & SONS BURSLEM.

13 H & Co BRIDEWOOD & SON ZELL AM

14 ANHERST JAPAN No 62 STONE CHINA

SHIELDS

1–2 Royal Factory, Vienna, Austria. Hard-paste porcelain. Painted blue. 1750–80.

3–5 Royal Factory, Vienna, Austria. Incised. 1744–1820.

6 Nymphenburg, Germany. Porcelain. 1754–1862.

7–8 Nymphenburg, Germany. c1800.

9 Ansbach, Germany. Hard-paste porcelain. Painted blue. Mid to late 18th C.

10 Wood & Barker, Burslem, England. 19th C.

11 Bridgwood & Son, Longton, England. 19th C.

12 Enoch Wood & Sons, Burslem, England. 1818–46.

13 Zell, Germany. Glazed earthenware. After 1818.

14 Stoke-on-Trent, England. Porcelain. c1799.

15 Copeland & Garrett, Spode, Stoke-on-Trent, England. 1833–47.

16 Minton, Stoke-on-Trent, England. After 1868.

SQUARES

1–4 Meissen, Germany. Bottger red stoneware. c1710–20.

5 John & David Elers (potters), Newcastle, England. Stoneware. c1690–1710.

6 Chelsea, London, England. Porcelain. 1745–85.

7–11 Worcester, England. Porcelain. Late 18th C.

12 Derby, England. Painted blue. c1775.

13–14 Bow, London, England. Mid 18th C.

15 Mayer & Newbold, Longton, Staffordshire, England. Painted red. 19th C.

16 Baden, Germany. Mid 18th C.

STARS AND SUNS

1 Isaac Farnsworth, Derby, England. 18th–19th C.

2/5/6 Ginori, Doccia, Italy. 1735–7.

3 Wallendorf, Thuringia, Germany. Porcelain. c1764.

4 'De Ster' (The Star), Delft, Holland. Faïence. c1690.

7 Caughley, England. Porcelain. c1750.

8 Nove, Italy. Faïence, porcelain. Painted gold. Mid 18th C.

9 Wedgwood, Etruria, England. Impressed. 1765–1850.

10 Nymphenburg, Germany. Hard-paste porcelain. Late 18th C.

11 Savona, Italy. 18th C.

12 Seville, Spain. 19th C.

13 Nevers, France. Faïence. 17th C.

14–15 St Cloud, France. Soft-paste porcelain. Painted blue. 1678–1766.

16 Robert Bloor, Derby, England. c1811–48.

14

15

16

TRIANGLES AND HEARTS

1–2 Chelsea, London, England. Soft-paste porcelain. Painted gold or red. c1745–50.

3–4 Bow, London, England. Incised. Painted blue. Mid 18th C.

5 Derby, England. Hard-paste porcelain. Impressed. Painted blue. Mid 18th C.

6 Bristol, England. Hard-paste porcelain. Impressed. c1763–73.

7 Sèvres, France. 1900–2. Mark tells year of decoration.

8 Meissen, Germany. Porcelain. Impressed. c1766–80.

9 Burslem, England. 19th C.

10 Sèvres, France. Hard-paste porcelain. Painted black. Soft-paste painted blue. c1900–11.

11 Hanley, England. 19th C.

12 Newcastle, England. 19th C.

13 Orleans, France. Hard and soft paste porcelain. Painted colour. c1753–1812.

14 Rue Popincourt factory, Paris, France. Porcelain. c1782–1835.

15 Richard Chaffers, Liverpool, England. c1740–65.

16 Bruges, Belgium. 18th C.

14   **15**   **16**

1

2

3

4

5

6

7

8

9

10

ORIENTAL COPIES

1–6 Worcester marks, 1751–83.
7 Caughley, England. c1772–99.
8 Burslem, England. Late 17th or early 18th C.
9–11 Meissen, Germany. Bottger ware. Early 18th C.
12 Samson 'the Imitator', Paris, France. Found on imitation Lowestoft (England). c1875.
13 Coalport, Coalbrookdale, England. Hard-paste porcelain c1828–50.
14 Delft, Holland. Faïence. Painted blue. c1800.
15 'De Romeyn' (The Roman), Delft, Holland. Faïence. c1671.

1. CAMPANIA — T. & R. BOOTE — ROYAL SEMI PORCELAIN — WARRANTED POTTERIES — ENGLAND

2. Prize Medal — T. & R. BOOTE.

3. Stevenson

4.

5.

6.

7.

8.

9.

10.

11.

12.

13.

14.

15.

16.

17.

18. Cambrian Pottery

19. SWANSEA LATE DILLWYN

20. MEDINA T.G.

21. OLD HALL — 1740

22.

23.

24.

MISCELLANEOUS

1–2 T & R Boote, Burslem, England. Late 18th C.

3 Cobridge, Staffordshire, England. Painted blue. c1800.

4 Delft, Holland. Faïence. 18th C.

5 'De Oude Moriaan's Hooft' (The Old Moor's Head), Delft, Holland. Faïence. c1680.

6 Royal Vienna Factory, Austria. c1850.

7 Derby, England. Hard-paste porcelain. Painted blue. 1745–1848.

8 Paris. Hard-paste porcelain. Painted gold. c1870.

9 Caughley, England. Porcelain. 1750–1814.

10 Clignancourt, France. Hard-paste porcelain. c1771–5.

11 Worcester, England. c1751–83.

12 Chantilly, France. Soft-paste porcelain. Painted blue or red. c1725–1800.

13 J & M P Bell & Co, Scotland. Late 19th C.

14 Limoges, France. Hard-paste porcelain. c1736–96.

15–16 Bellevue Pottery Co, Hull, England. Earthenware. c1825.

17 Savona, Italy. 17th C.

18 Cambrian factory, Swansea, Wales. Soft-paste porcelain. c1765.

19 W T Copeland & Sons, Spode, Stoke-on-Trent, England. Porcelain. c1847.

20 Burslem, England. c1795.

21 Old Hall Pottery, England. Earthenware. 19th C.

22 Tournay, Belgium. Soft-paste porcelain, late 18th C.

23 Clignancourt, France. Hard-paste. Painted blue, gold. c1771–98.

24 Savona, Italy. 18th C.

25–27 Bristol, England. Pottery, porcelain. Painted blue or gold. 18th C.

28 Nevers, France. Pottery. Painted colour. 16th C.

29–31 Plymouth, England. Hard-paste porcelain. Painted red, blue or gold. c1768.

32–34 Royal Factory, Berlin, Germany. Hard-paste porcelain. Painted blue. c1760.

35 Hanley, England. 19th C.

36 Nymphenburg, Germany. Porcelain. Impressed or incised. Late 18th C.

37 Caughley, England. Hard-paste porcelain. Painted blue. c1750.

38 Bow, London, England. Porcelain. c1750.

39 Bristol, England. Hard-paste porcelain. Painted colour. c1770.

40 Bristol, England. Hard-paste porcelain. Printed blue. c1800.

41 Job Ridgways (potter), Shelton, England. c1794.

42 Podmore, Walker & Co, Staffordshire, England. c1755.

41   42

5. Oriental porcelain

The marks that appear on Chinese and Japanese wares are quite different from their Western counterparts – and not merely in the matter of script. When European traders began importing Chinese porcelain in the 15th and 16th centuries, it was assumed that the marks indicated the names of the makers. British and European potters and factories accordingly followed suit, each maker displaying his own mark. In fact, Chinese marks do not refer to potters at all, but either indicate the emperor in whose reign a piece was made, or represent symbols of good omen or commendation.

False Marks
Identifying oriental porcelain by its marks alone is difficult and potentially risky. The marks often imitate those of earlier periods, either as a gesture of respect towards ancestors, or as simple forgery. The accurate identification of oriental ware requires above all a knowledge of period and factory styles – the marks can be regarded, at best, as a back-up.

CHINESE PORCELAIN
Porcelain was a Chinese discovery and its manufacture dates back to the 9th century AD, although other forms of pottery have been found in China dating from many centuries earlier. The great periods for Chinese porcelain are generally considered to be the reigns of the Ming and the Ch'ing Emperors, at the beginning of which porcelain became fashionable.

Reading Chinese marks

Chinese script reads in columns from right to left. Most marks consist of two columns of three characters each. To read them, go from top to bottom of the right-hand column, then top to bottom of the left.

The first two characters signify the word 'great' (ta) (**1**), followed by the name of the dynasty (**2**). The next two characters represent the reign-name – usually the Emperor's first and second names (**3**, **4**). The final two are 'period' (nien) (**5**) and 'make' (chih) (**6**).

(There was also a dating system based on a 60-year cycle, using two symbols, but these alternative marks were rarely applied and are difficult to interpret.)

In marks where there are only four characters, the dynasty is omitted. There is also an alternative form consisting of a square seal mark, written in an archaic script known as 'seal character'.

Example of a six-character mark

Ming dynasty
Lung Ch'ing (Longqing) 1567–72

Principal Chinese Dynasties

Dynasty	Dates
Shang Yin	1760–1120 BC
Chou	1120–249 BC
Ch'in	221–206 BC
Han	206 BC–AD 220
Six Dynasties	AD 220–589
T'ang	AD 618–906
Five Dynasties	AD 907–960
Sung	AD 960–1279
Yuan	AD 1279–1367
Ming	AD 1368–1644
Ch'ing	AD 1644–1916

Ming and Ch'ing (Qing) dynasties

These two dynasties are the most important as regards Chinese porcelain. The Ming dynasty was established in 1368 and consisted of 17 reigns, ending in 1644. Power then passed to the Ch'ing (Qing) dynasty, which consisted of 11 reigns and lasted until 1916.

Ming means 'bright' and Ch'ing (Qing) means 'pure'.

Ming dynasty reign marks

1 Hung-wu (Hongwu), 1368–98
2 Chien-wen, 1399–1402
3a Yung-lo (Yongle), 1403–24
3b (in archaic script)
4 Hung-hsi, 1425

5a Hsuan-te (Xuande), 1426–35
5b (in seal characters)
6 Cheng-t'ung, 1436–49
7 Ching-t'ai, 1450–57
8 T'ien-shun, 1457–64
9a Ch'eng-hua, 1465–87
9b (in seal characters)

10 Hung-chih (Hongzhi),
1488–1505

11 Cheng-te (Zhengde),
1506–21

12 Chia-ching (Jiajing),
1522–66

13 Lung-ch'ing
(Longqing), 1567–72

14 Wan-li (Wanli),
1573–1619

15 T'ai-ch'ang (1620)

16 Tien-ch'i (Tianqi),
1621–27

17 Ch'ung-cheng
(Chongzhen), 1628–43

10 治年製

大明弘

11 德年製

大明正

12 靖年製

大明嘉

13 慶年製

大明隆

14 曆年製

大明萬

15 泰昌

16 啟年製年製

大明天崇禎

17

Ch'ing (Qing) dynasty
1a Shun-chih (Shunzhi), 1644–61
1b (in seal characters)
2 K'ang-hsi (Kangxi), 1662–1722
3a Yung-cheng (Yongzheng), 1723–35

3b (in seal characters)
4a Ch'ien-lung (Qianlong), 1736–95
4b (in seal characters)
5a Chia-ch'ing (Jiaqing), 1796–1821
5b (in seal characters)

1a 治年製 大清順

3a 正年製 大清雍

4b (seal characters)

1b (seal characters)

3b (seal characters)

5a 年製 嘉慶

2 熙年製 大清康

4a 隆年製 大清乾

5b (seal characters)

6 Tao-kung (Daoguang), 1821–50

7a Hsien-feng (Xianfeng), 1851–61

7b (in seal characters)

8a T'ung-chih (Tongzhi), 1862–73

8b (in seal characters)

9a Kuang-hsu (Guangxu), 1874–1908

9b (in seal characters)

10 Hsuan-t'ung (Xuantong), 1909–12

11 Hung-hsien (Hongxian), 1916

6
大清道光年製

7a
大清咸豐年製

7b

8a
大清治年製

8b

9a
大清光緒年製

9b

10
大清統年製

11
大清宣年製洪憲

JAPANESE PORCELAIN

Porcelain was first made in Japan in the early 17th century, beginning with the early Arita wares. Decoration, especially for export to Europe, often followed the Chinese style. However, there are a number of distinctive Japanese styles, among them Imari with its popular vivid red, blue and gilded vases and dishes; Kakiemon, with its beautiful enamel decoration; and Nabeshima, which used delicate underglaze blue and enamel decoration.

Japanese marks

Japanese marks are even more unreliable than Chinese ones. They include not only copies of Chinese marks, but names of potters, patrons and places. However, much of the best Japanese porcelain bears no marks at all, and very few marks appear before the end of the 18th century.

A few common examples of Japanese marks have been included here for reference.

'Raku' seal

'Kenzan' signature

'Banko' seal

Two forms of 'fuku'
(meaning happiness)

'Kutani'

Impressed
signature of 'Ninsei'

COLLINS GEM

Bestselling Collins Gem titles include:

Gem English Dictionary (£3.50)

Gem Calorie Counter (£2.99)

Gem Thesaurus (£3.50)

Gem French Dictionary (£3.50)

Gem German Dictionary (£3.50)

Gem Basic Facts Mathematics (£3.50)

Gem Birds Photoguide (£3.99)

Gem Babies' Names (£3.50)

Gem Card Games (£3.50)

Gem World Atlas (£3.50)

All Collins Gems are available from your local bookseller or can be ordered directly from the publishers.

In the UK, contact Mail Order, Dept 2A, HarperCollins Publishers, Westerhill Rd, Bishopbriggs, Glasgow, G64 2QT, listing the titles required and enclosing a cheque or p.o. for the value of the books plus £1.00 for the first title and 25p for each additional title to cover p&p. Access and Visa cardholders can order on 0141-772 2281 (24 hr).

In Australia, contact Customer Services, HarperCollins Distribution, Yarrawa Rd, Moss Vale 2577 (tel. [048] 68 0300). **In New Zealand**, contact Customer Services, HarperCollins Publishers, 31 View Rd, Glenfield, Auckland 10 (tel. [09] 444 3740). **In Canada**, contact your local bookshop.

All prices quoted are correct at time of going to press.